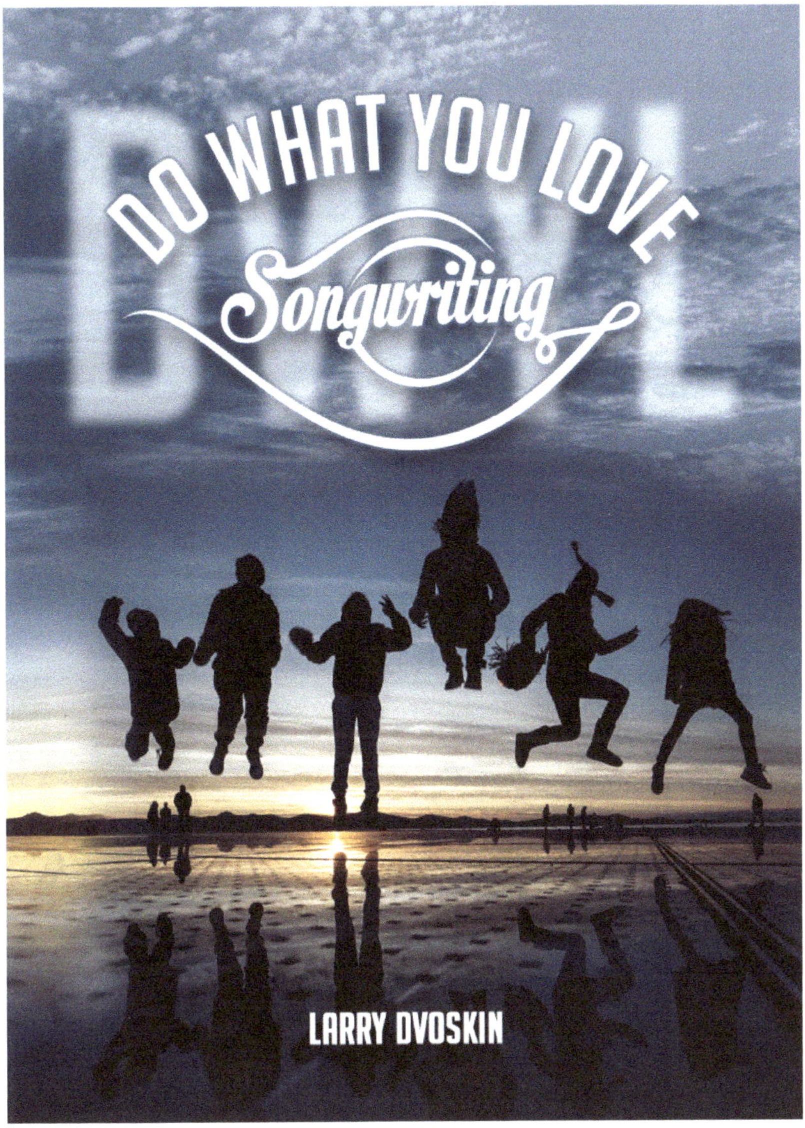
DWYL
DO WHAT YOU LOVE
Songwriting
LARRY DVOSKIN

Larry Dvoskin
Do What You Love: Songwriting

Published by Do What You Love Media, LLC
© 2015 and © 2017 and © 2020 by Larry Dvoskin

All rights reserved, including the right to reproduce this book or portions thereof in any form whatsoever. For further information and requests, please email: todayisthefuture@gmail.com

ISBN: 978-0-9968792-1-7
ISBN: 978-0-9968792-2-4

Manufactured in the United States of America

Cover design by Igor Prole; http://www.igorprole.com
(Teenage wasteland, playing keyboards in Fandango (1981). Artwork by Jesse Siminski.)

TABLE OF CONTENTS

DEDICATION 5
FOREWORD 7
ACKNOWLEDGEMENTS 9
INTRODUCTION 11
CHAPTER 1. Good Leads to Better 13
   Life Is Strange 15
CHAPTER 2. Follow Your Joy 21
   Everyone's A Hooker 23
CHAPTER 3. Be Audacious 27
   The King of Trite 30
   Each One of Us 40
CHAPTER 4. See Life as Energy 45
   Love Heels 47
   Brothers and Sisters 56
CHAPTER 5. Travel 63
   The Only Thing Missing 66
   Reflexology 70
CHAPTER 6. Be of Service 73
   Journey Through Life 78
CHAPTER 7. Trust Yourself 83
   I Can't Hold You Forever 84
CHAPTER 8. Embrace the Negative! 91
   Live It All 93
AFTERWORD 99
Glossary of Terms 101

DEDICATION

This book is dedicated to all of those dreamers who have a song in their heart and a story to tell. We each endeavor in the hours of the days to fulfill our potential by doing what we love.

This book is also dedicated to my mother Shirley Friedman Dvoskin who taught me that being happy is the most important thing in life.

FOREWORD

Larry Dvoskin is a teacher of the process of songwriting in this wonderful new book Do What You Love-Songwriting. He uses his own whimsical and musically brilliant album, "Life is Strange," as a template to inspire. He describes what he calls the "eight keys of Do What You Love" in the process, and uses each track of the album to exemplify that process.

My first memories of Larry as a songwriter begin here in Big Sur California in the 1990's, where we co-wrote a half dozen songs together in a matter of hours. Everything in our environment was an inspiration, which is an important part of the process.

Larry is such a prolific songwriter that he reminds me of Brian Wilson in the early days of the Beach Boys, of which I am a founding member.

I remember coming home one day after going to town and finding Larry sitting on a fence serenading our cow named Jennifer. He was so taken by the beauty of the beast, he couldn't help himself.

That was about 20 years ago, and we are still in the process of doing the vocals for that song now titled "Jenny Clover." It's one of my favorites. I always say, if an idea is good it's good forever. Don't give up on it. That could be another key Larry, to Do What You Love.

- Al Jardine
- Rock and Roll Hall of Fame inductee
- Grammy lifetime award recipient
- Co-founding member of The Beach Boys

ACKNOWLEDGEMENTS

To all of the students at New York University who have taken the Songwriting course that I teach. I have learned as much from you and perhaps even more, than you may have learned from the course.

To Igor Prole who designed the book cover which everyone loves. Y'all should hire him for your next project!

To all of the editors who helped correct my lousy spelling and bring balance to this literary litany.

To famed aviator Charles Lindbergh who's Spirit of St. Louis flies within my soul, and whose wings dented the 20th century and changed the world. May he fly in peaceful blue skies forever more. To Al and Mary Ann Jardine who have been amongst the most loving, and supportive friends of my lifetime.

To those composers that inspire me including The Lennon's, Irving Berlin, and JS Bach.

INTRODUCTION

THE EIGHT KEYS OF DO WHAT YOU LOVE – SONGWRITING

I have been stalling. For years people have told me that I describe the unexplainable process of writing songs in a clear, simple, accessible way and that I ought to write a book about it. I have also been accused of having too much fun in life, as if joy is a crime. I've heard many times that others would benefit if I would spill the beans and just share my secrets. So, I have finally gotten around to it…and you are holding the results: Do What You Love – Songwriting.

The eight keys of Do What You Love are a multi-colored tapestry of life lessons. Woven together they form a mindset that I have embraced and share with you for living life to the fullest. They embody commonalities I have found in my quest for wisdom and enlightenment across time and platform…from religion to philosophy, from "how to" common sense, to mysticism. Learning as much from challenge and failure, as from success.

I wrap a personal experience around each key that led to the creation of a song. It could be a *good leads to better* song, or an *embrace the negative* story. It's a bit complicated to tie three diverse tent poles of a book together, and perhaps wiser, greater men would have split them off into separate books. Not me.

But this is what makes Do What You Love unique. No other music resource to my understanding shares a real life story with a life lesson philosophy that demonstrates how it led to a creative breakthrough. No other personal development book is directly tied to a creative work and deconstructs the behind the scenes mechanisms to how it was brought to life.

Albert Einstein is famously is quoted as saying "The tragedy of life is what dies inside a man while he lives." On the following pages are many stories of how I let out the music inside me. This is my sharing the keys to help you unlock the mysterious force inside each and every one of us.

THE EIGHT KEYS:

1. Good Leads to Better
2. Follow Your Joy
3. Be Audacious!
4. See Life as Energy
5. Travel
6. Service to Others
7. Trust Yourself
8. Embrace the Negative

Do What You Love – Songwriting focuses on how one can turn their passion for songwriting, into a career. I have walked the talk my entire life. In the following pages I share my secrets so that you can endeavor to do it too. No matter how old you are, no matter where you live, no matter what contacts you have or may not have, no matter your proficiency on a musical instrument.

This book is about how life, art, science and physics are all interconnected. We are each an instrument in the orchestra of the universe. We each have a special moment when it's our turn to shine. I hope that what I share with you helps the creativity in you to grow. . As a career musician and songwriter, that is the basis of this first installment of what will become an ongoing Do What You Love series. Music is love. Our songs spread like ripples on the water far and wide after we're gone. They live. They grow. They last forever.

Each one of us has our own unique stories to tell. Here are a few of mine.

CHAPTER 1. GOOD LEADS TO BETTER

Life is like a train. Good leads to better and bad leads to worse, so get on the good train.

It's a law of physics: Whatever we focus on gets bigger. If the news programs or websites are all negative, then turn away from them. You're allowed! I hereby give you permission to go on a "media fast." Similar to a food fast, you may now consider abstaining from so many negative current event "calories" each day.

MY "GOOD LEADS TO BETTER" STORY

I was in the full bloom of youth when I wrote the song "Life Is Strange" in 1979. I was just leaving the RCA signed group Fandango to be managed as a solo performer by Bud Prager, who was at the time New York's most successful rock manager. I was living the dream of a young musician, and good kept leading to better. I went from being the unathletic, uncool kid in high school to joining Fandango and having my picture in *Rolling Stone* magazine, touring the world, making a living, traveling, and enjoying the fulfillment and stability of a real life dream job. Shortly after Fandango broke up, I stepped out of my role of side man and into the role of front man by writing songs and playing with my own band. I wrote the song "Life Is Strange" as a self challenge to write a carnival-type piece with "Being for the Benefit of Mr. Kite" by The Beatles serving as it's inspiration.

In 1981, I went to see my first Fellini film, "City Of Women." It was playing at an art house cinema near Lincoln Square in New York City. It was a crazy film yet the audience looked to me like the sophisticated, upscale people you'd see at the opera. I'd never seen anything like it. The film was surreal, creative, naughty, edgy, a whole world of things. I went home and wrote this song.

When I first presented "Life Is Strange" to manager Bud Prager, he just kind of looked at me and scratched his head. He said that, to him it was genius, but he didn't quite know what to do with it. His taste at the time leaned toward huge hits like the ones his group Foreigner was cranking out at the time: classic rock standards like "Hot Blooded," "Feels Like The First Time," and "Waiting for a Girl Like You." My song was a weirdo in comparison.

Bud wasn't alone. I also didn't know what to do so I put it away. But every once in a while when I'd play it at parties or social gatherings, people went crazy for it. From the first chorus, people would sing along with the words "Life is strange, life is strange." It was operatic, like Queen's "Bohemian Rhapsody," and you didn't need a Ph.D. to follow it.

Ten years after I had written it and had played it for a friend, I ran into him in another city and he said to me, "Hey, whatever happened to that song 'Life Is Strange'?" He then proceeded to sing it to me. The fact that he could recall it ten years later was a clear sign the universe was telling me that I needed to record it and share it with the world.

To this day, that refrain has a resonance. Life is *still* strange, in fact! Look around: Maybe life has become even stranger?

LIFE IS STRANGE

Words and Music by Larry Dvoskin

The nipsy gypsy thought it was hip
She abandoned ship, she couldn't swim
The rolly polly prayed to the holy
Guacamole, God named Jim
I Feel Like I'm Living In a Salvador Dali Painting
I Feel like a Fellini Star In a Movie That's Gone Too far
Life Is Strange, Life Is Strange
Life Is strange, Life Is Strange
The cock star rock star looked like a lobster
With a rooster's head, and fish nosed beak
The Gucci poochi of Fiorucci's
Changed her sex so she'd look chic
I Feel Like I'm Living In a Salvador Dali Painting
I Feel like a Fellini Star In a Movie That's Gone Too far
Life Is Strange, Life Is Strange
Life Is strange, Life Is strange
All day long they dress in their normal suits pretending they are sane
But when they're alone they think naughty thoughts like vulgar insects
In their brain
Romulus Bomulus read existentialist
Books in his hotel of doubt
Spartacus Articus just laughed at this
Whole world as he checked out

THE SONG DECONSTRUCTION

One of my favorite lines that I've ever written is in this chorus where the lyric states, "I Feel Like I'm Living In A Salvador Dali Painting." This sums up life to me. It's amazing, wonderful, horrible, and surreal at times. This line sticks.

The bridge lyric portraying normal people sitting behind their desks, looking and acting sane while inside their brain are thoughts "like vulgar insects," for me, was the pure art expression I was aiming for:

"All day long they dress in their normal suits pretending they are sane. But when they're alone they think naughty thoughts like vulgar insects in their brain."

The second verse reference to the cock star rock star is both narcissistic and autobiographical. A friend I recently reconnected with who knew me back in the day described me as "precocious." In my teens and twenties, I had a Rod Stewart shag hairstyle, a record deal … and enjoyed the pleasures of the day perhaps a little too much at times? The "Gucci Poochie of Fiorucci's" was a whole crowd of people I had met at Studio 54. They all seemed so fashionable, chic, and fabulous, and at Studio, everyone I met was named "Francisco," or "Francesca," or "Francoise." Nobody seemed to be named "Bill" or "Bob." It was pretentiousness I was aiming for, as if a sex change was as casual as a manicure.

In the last verse, "Sparticus Articus" was a reference to a name I'd heard from the Sex Pistols. Upon researching for this book however, I couldn't find a direct explanation. However, it refers to It's a strange character that is on the edge of society. He finally decides he's had enough of life and checks out. The whole last verse, dry in production, points to our aging and loss of innocence – the time when suddenly weird isn't that much fun anymore. We grow more fragile and cautious having been beaten down by life's events. Both Spartacus and Romulus are historical characters from Roman history or mythology.

MELODY

The main title line at the end of the chorus demonstrates my "dramatic leap" concept that memorable melodies can often embody a major leap of notes. "Life Is Strange" is "Somewhere Over The Rainbow" in reverse. In the latter, the first word "Somewhere" leaps an octave up. In "Life Is Strange", it drops down an octave. It creates a musical headline, much in the way we see a newspaper headline in large bold print. The huge leap of notes is the musical equivalent of a large typeface.

Also, the chorus melody "I feel like I'm living" starts with a major 7th note. It's a very sweet-sounding note against a pretty chord, but the twist is a strange lyric line attached.

I've always endeavored to write a bridge that breaks loose from the rest of the song – kind of like in the Beatles' "I Am The Walrus," with the bridge "sitting in an English garden waiting for the sun…" The bridge in "Life Is Strange" goes off the rails into strange, unrelated musical territory and lyrics.

CHORDS

This song presents a classic example of minor chords in the verse – A minor, E – to major chords in the chorus – F major 7th, G, etc. These chords are related, but the minor to major switcheroo gives the song a noticeable lift and separates the sound of the sections.

ARRANGEMENT

This is a fairly classic pop song arrangement, but with many production twists and turns. Here's why:

It starts with a short four – bar intro, verse one, chorus one, verse two, chorus two. Then it shakes things up with the bridge section; one line that both the melody and band follows "All day long", and it truly takes the song into the land of strange. It exemplifies it. Songs like "Sunshine of Your Love" and others where the vocal and musical riffs are together in unison influenced this.

After this bridge comes a solo section with honky-tonk piano and echoed voices from each speaker. I was heavily influenced by Pink Floyd, and their recordings often embodied voices within their songs: muffled things you could barely make out. Toward the end you hear "the doors of perception were opening." This refers to the band the Doors. After that is a symphony gone wild playing some melodic notes. This was my Beatles' "Your Mother Should Know" moment, only I added in some wild cymbal crashes and backward instruments so it takes off on its own and tries to behave, but the song simply can't.

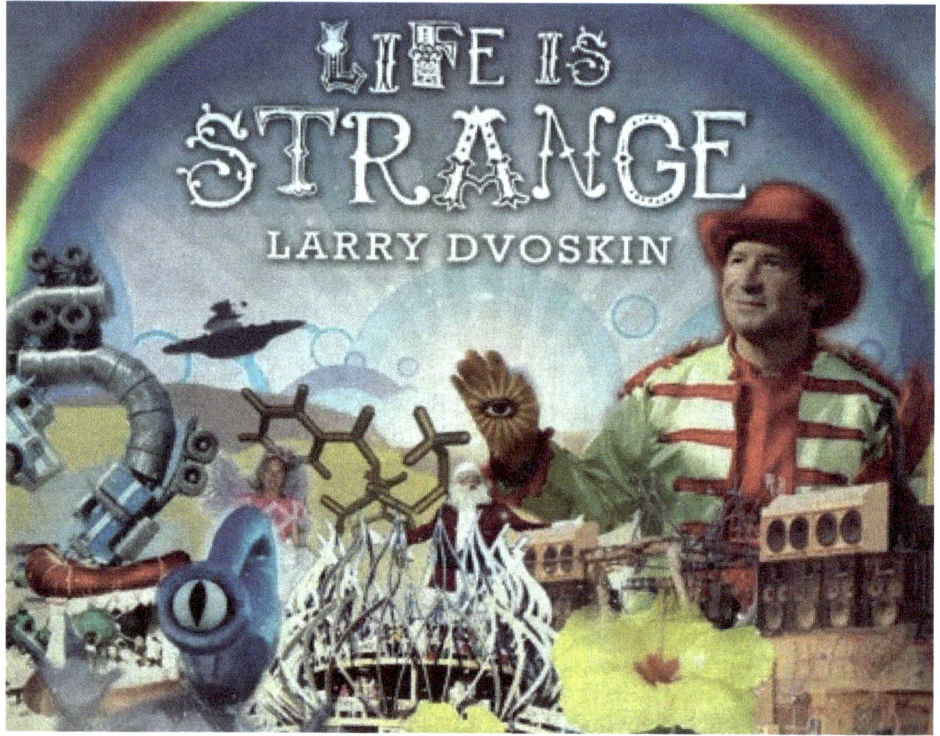

Cover art "Life Is Strange" album

Also in this last musical bridge section, the bass line runs almost chromatically down while the melody goes up. This came from my classical training and Bach influence. Bach often wrote fugues where the two hands would run melodically in opposite directions but in counterpoint harmony to each other. The Beatles often employed this intuitively via Paul's bass playing, and George Martin's classical training helped amplify this concept.

PRODUCTION

Often times I explain in my NYU classes that I have had to record and re-record a song many times until it's right. There is no guarantee for magic. It just happens. I started recording it with a friend who simply couldn't get the "oompa" feel of a Bavarian beer hall. He just couldn't "oompa."

Then I threw it over to another programmer friend, and another. I added keyboards and vocals myself at home in New York. It gradually came together. I had gangs of friends come over and shout "Life Is Strange" around the mic to create a crowd sound. I simply experimented a lot and let it ripen with age like a fine wine.

When it was time to mix, it took me hiring and firing several different studios until it felt right. It couldn't be too 'reverby', as it was circuslike, yet couldn't be too dry or it would sound flat. Different sections came to life via completely different approaches. The solo piano section needed lots of reverb and the background voices to be panned and kind of dreamlike. The last verse has to be very dry and crisp, as if the narrator has come back to Earth, waking up to reality. Lyrically, the last verse points to "checking out" when life gets too difficult.

I don't know if I could have pulled off all the nuanced production when I was younger and originally wrote it. It might have just sounded like a progressive rock band sloshing through a carnival-type song. Instead, the experience that comes with age allowed me to really hone it until it exemplified the sound I was hearing in my head. And with age I also had the financing to keep working on it until it was right.

Record your own notes here:

CHAPTER 2. FOLLOW YOUR JOY

───

Sometimes it takes years of trying, doing, training, investing, going for broke in order to find success.

Apple started in Steve Jobs' garage with a $1,500 investment. The Beatles played for five years in Hamburg for little or no pay in shitty conditions. They were simply following their hearts' desire doing what they loved before the big break came.

"The only way to do great work is to love what you do. If you haven't found it yet, keep looking. Don't settle." – Steve Jobs

"When you rise in the morning, give thanks for the light, for your life, for your strength. Give thanks for your food and for the joy of living. If you see no reason to give thanks, the fault lies in yourself." – Tecumseh

MY "FOLLOW YOUR JOY" STORY

In 2009, I was the patriarch of a soul family of friends, a ringleader for a merry bunch of *twenty somethings* in New York City. All were gifted and like bright little fireflies they shone and made their way in the urban jungle that is Gotham to explore and hopefully live their dreams. Around that time I watched an interview with Arnold Schwarzenegger.

The reporter was trying to anger him by suggesting that Arnold wasn't an actor; that he just flashed his muscles while waving a gun and that, indeed, he was nothing more than a high-paid hooker. Arnold replied in his thick Austrian accent, "Well, all us actors are like prostitutes. We create a fantasy that isn't real."

I marveled that even though politics and what some call *the world's oldest profession* are very similar, the former governor of California went so far as to compare his actor self to a hooker. This got me thinking about the commerce of give and take, that we each have a pure part of our souls that we trade to make a living.

Video shoot for "Everyone's a Hooker" (2010)

This period was a fantastic time in my life. I was doing what I love, following my joy, eating well, full of health and energy. In addition to acting as a curator of a salon of creative, younger performers, I was also teaching at NYU. Since following your joy is a decision and good leads to better, the making of "Life Is Strange", my first real solo album, was a creative bucket list gift to myself. "Everyone's A Hooker" was the last song to go on "Life Is Strange".

I was trying to tell a symbolic story about the dark side of capitalism and the erosion of the American dream.

EVERYONE'S A HOOKER

Words and Music by: Larry Dvoskin and Zoe Silverman

All my friends are hookers
Drug addicts good lookers
All f**ked up broken again
The doorbell rings – at 4am
Buying and selling your 'wares' on the street
Gotta make some cash, gotta make ends meet
Pay the rent, the bills, the electricity
I get something from you, you get something from me
Everyone's A Hooker
Everyone, Everyone, Every, Every, Everyone
Everyone's A Hooker
Dark secret skeletons hustling on the sly
F**kin' your boss selling 'trees' on the side
Teachers and preachers politicians and musicians
Doctors and lawyers and we're all peep show voyeurs
Everyone's A Hooker
Everyone, Everyone, Every, Every, Everyone
Everyone's A Hooker
Welcome to the American Dream
There's a hidden price for liberty
The streets aren't paved with gold you see
If you wanna eat better hit the streets cause
Everyone, Everyone, Everyone, Everyone Yeah
Everyone, Everyone, Everyone, Everyone Yeah
(insert orgy here)
I'm on 6th Avenue gotta make that green
Selling cheap incense and burned CD's
When all I really want is to be on TV
Cause Everyone….

THE SONG DECONSTRUCTION

"All my friends are hookers, drug addicts, good lookers"

Now that's a wallop for a pop single…and a confession, if somewhat an exaggeration. The intro starts out with a very sappy, tongue-in-cheek melody against major 7th chords. This is designed to throw off the listener from the salacious lyric.

The verses don't do much melodically, but just as in "No Scrubs" by TLC, the short and sharp rhythm of the melody is the hook. The melody of "Hooker" has a staccato pattern that also is its own hook.

CHORUS

The "get to the chorus; don't bore us" formula is at work here. Repeat the title, mash it up half way through, "everyone, everyone, everyone"…It's just very simple and easy to remember.

SECOND VERSE

I credit a lot of edgy street terminology to the composition's co-writer Zoe Silverman, then just twenty-years old. She talked about selling trees, meaning pot, and having sex with your boss.

I have always loved list songs, since John Lennon wrote lots of word list lyrics a la "Give Peace a Chance," so the "doctors and lawyers and we're all peep show voyeurs" is my moment to expand the concept that everyone who has to make a living, is sacrificing some part of themselves. Be it time, intelligence, musical skills, or a great set of hips.

ARRANGEMENT

Most of the song is just A major to D major; two chords. The only main switch is to A minor and D major in the bridge.

Also in the bridge, it changes tempo and genre. I loved this approach, which I developed being a musical child of the 1970s. Music was adventurous. Songs might change tempo, or key, or go through a metamorphosis. So the track goes from a reggae beat to a rock & roll bridge. The bridge starts to build and rise. It was influenced by the orchestral rise in "A Day in the Life" by the Beatles. I wanted the bridge of "Hooker" to go off the rails, to explode. The song gets louder and wilder with the screams and groans.

Cast & Crew of "Everyone's A Hooker"

The ending is about the failure of being a hooker, and for that matter, more often than not, a musician as well. The last line, "all I really want is to be on T.V." sums up our collective experience worshipping celebrities and fame. With YouTube and other online platforms, everyone can now have their five seconds of fame.

It's a statement of how we have begun to worship the golden calf of our own making.

POP SECRET #1: 1, MINOR 6, 4, 5

(Flood the neuro-receptors with sounds that release serotonin)

The chord progression "1, minor 6, 4, 5" is one of the most commonly-used chord progressions, across decades, genres, types of songs, styles of music. It just rings our bell.

When I first became a musician I never stopped to realize that "Heart and Soul," "Stand by Me", "Every Breath You Take," are exactly the same chords. Amazing! And there are countless other evergreen hits and more recent ones like "Baby" by Justin Bieber that use the same chord pattern.

My own theory is that our reptilian brain, developed over eons, is wary of unfamiliar sights, sounds, smells, and more open to something it recognizes. Think about it: That shadow behind the tree could be a tiger waiting to pounce and eat us, or it could just be a harmless shadow. What we don't know might hurt us, but what we recognize allows us to let our guard down. It's true for sight, touch, taste, smell, as well as music, which is sound.

For non-music readers or lyricists, this means in the key of C major, the chords would be C, A minor, F, G. In the key of G major, it's G, E minor, C, D. It transposes easily. If we mash up the sequence a little, say we play 1, 5, minor 6, 4, then we suddenly get a whole other series of hits like U2's "With or Without You", or Lady Gaga's "Paparazzi."

Now, I don't believe for a second that Bono or Lady Gaga sat down and said to themselves, "I'm going to write a classic hit that uses 1, 5, minor 6, 4 to ride the neuro-receptor waves." It's more subconscious than that. After tens of thousands of hours of hearing, playing, writing, and recording music, the creative juices just flow down this river naturally. What this means for those of you who don't have a musical vocabulary is you're now aware of an important musical pattern, which can be used to relate to a songwriting collaborator when the music you are hearing isn't quite ringing your bell. It's the sound of "kaa-ching."

CHAPTER 3. BE AUDACIOUS

Steve Jobs advised the Stanford University graduating class of 2005 during his historic commencement speech to "Stay foolish."

Some of my best experiences in life, some of my biggest career breaks, have come from taking potentially embarrassing risks or actions that seemed to make no sense at the time. It was in these moments that breakthroughs often arrived from somewhere completely out of the blue.

It's as if by traveling, doing fun things, focusing on positive things that this letting go of routine creates a space for something new and wonderful that can fill it.

MY "BE AUDACIOUS" STORY

My cold call to the biggest music manager in New York around 1980 resulted in my whole life changing for the better. There are several sayings that are all well-worn clichés, but for the most part are true.

1. Successful people feel the fear and take action anyway.
2. Jump off the cliff and you grow wings on the way down.

(I did both by simply being audacious!)

As mentioned previously, I was in the RCA rock band Fandango, but after three moderately-successful albums I was looking to spread my wings and fly solo around 1980. I was very much a self-starter. Naturally what some would call a connector, I'd cold call people in the music business, make new friends, and attend social events along the way.

A very mischievous young man; "Last Kiss" album cover by Fandango, RCA Records (1979)

One day whilst leafing through a private insider industry magazine called *New on the Charts* I came across a listing of managers for bands currently on the Billboard charts. Among then was Bud Prager who managed Foreigner, one of the biggest-selling rock groups at the time. He previously also managed not one but two bands that performed at The Woodstock Festival of 1969: Mountain and Cream. For a young rock & roller like I was back then, it was like going off to seek the Wizard of Oz.

I just cold called Mr. Prager. The receptionist who answered was rude and had the attitude of "how dare you call the great and powerful

Oz!" I explained I was a young performer about to leave the RCA group Fandango and was looking to go solo and find a manager.

After I was briefly on hold, Mr. Prager got on the call. He told me my timing was remarkably synchronistic. He was just reading a letter from an old childhood friend who said something to the effect of "Bud, I've known you for all these years. You always need a mountain to climb to be happy. Now that Foreigner is the No. 1 group in the world, someone new is going to just call you up and say 'Hello, I'm so and so and I want you to manage me.'"

Bud told me that at that exact moment, his assistant had interrupted him to say, "Some young kid named Larry is on the phone from the group Fandango," and a light went on in his mind. So, even before I went up to his office I somehow knew he would become my manager.

Bud had an office at the top floor of 1790 Broadway in New York City. To me, a young teenage kid still living at home with my family, it was intimidating. The walls of his plush office were covered from floor to ceiling with gold and platinum disc awards. And, they weren't just any gold awards. They were to me some of the coolest rock artists in history: Cream, Clapton, Mountain, Woodstock 1969, and of course, Foreigner.

A year later when my contract was running out, and Bud was set to get on a private jet and circle the globe on a world tour with Foreigner. I took a big gamble and wrote this potentially offensive song. The surprisingly cynical and satirical lyrics are about the entire music industry, and my personal relationship with Bud (where I had to come into the office every week to play him my latest songs, or I wouldn't receive a check). It could just have easily backfired.

His album at the time, Foreigner 4, had the huge hit "Waiting for a Girl Like You" on it, and he could have simply sent me away, back home to the minor leagues to join the others struggling in the business.

Instead I spoke my truth, and my contract option and weekly salary was renewed, enabling me to "Do What I Love," – stay home and write songs.

THE KING OF TRITE

Words and Music by: Larry Dvoskin

He's the Wednesday is Sunday of songwriting/singers
buy one get one free
he's a discount house of music and sound
robotized by E.S.P
He flashes away like a pinball arcade with lines we all know
he's the prince of rhyme working overtime
a one man traveling show
He's The King of Trite – the new sensation
The King of Trite – sweeping the nation
he's the king the mighty, he's the one and only king
Mommy and daddy drop us off in the concert parking lot
we stand on our seats to get a glimpse
of the God we worship on our I-pods
He's The King of Trite – the new sensation
The King of Trite – sweeping the nation
wheeling around like a circus clown
blinded in the lines he sings
he's the man holding the noose tight around his neck
he's the puppet they'll cut loose, falling, falling to his end
He's The King of Trite – the new sensation
The King of Trite – sweeping the nation
on his FM throne the king of rock and roll
but the music died so long ago.

THE SONG DECONSTRUCTION

"He's the Wednesday is Sunday of songwriting/singers;

buy one get one free".

People frequently complain about the bad state of music these days that it used to be better in the good-old days. What good-old days are we thinking of? Bach's period? The 1920s? I wrote this line around 1981, feeling that the best popular music was already behind us.

On television during that time there was an ad for Carvel ice cream. It said that on each Wednesday, you could buy one ice cream cake and get a second one free. So the phrase came from a very annoying, yet popular commercial. The idea was undervaluing something, commercializing it.

This song was my rebellion against corporate rock – how musical artists went from creating freely, to attaching themselves to record companies that were simply signing up 100 groups that look and sound the same, throwing them against the wall in the hope that one or two might stick.

"The King of Trite" was literally, a "fuck you" to Bud Prager! His talent company was called ESP Management, his namesake birth initials: "He's a discount house of music and sound, robotized by ESP."

I was being audacious, precocious. Bud saw the truth in it. I was writing about a much larger cultural phenomenon from my own experience. It touched a nerve when I wrote this song.

BRIDGE LYRIC

"He's the man holding the noose tight around his neck, he's the puppet they'll cut loose, falling, falling to his end."

These lines simply reminded me of the fragility of fame. Andy Warhol once said everyone will get fifteen minutes of fame in their lifetime. Now, that time is about two seconds. One day you're on top of the world, the next you are yesterday's news. It can be heartbreaking.

MELODY

Because the lyrics are quite image-orientated, the melody is quite simple in the verses. The main thing melodically that stands out is the bold headline leap in the chorus. The words "King of Trite" jump a 5th. It's a leap, and as we keep discussing these bold headline-type leaps grab the listener's ear. Also, the simple hits at the end of each verse section and end of the chorus create a hook, "he's the king the mighty, he's the one and only king." Even though the melody stays on the chord and doesn't move much, it hits bombastically with the drums, bass and guitar creating a rhythmic hook.

ARRANGEMENT

At the time, there were some very original artistic rock bands with huge hit records. I was highly influenced by them, especially the bombastic arrangements of Queen and the Who. They'd do tempo changes, break into strange theatrical interludes, and do lots of drum fills and crashes rather than the straight-ahead, everything-is-at-the same-volume-and-tempo music that comprises a majority of pop music we hear today.

I liked this classical rock approach so I chose to write "The King of Trite" as if it were a rock song in this more bombastic style.

PRODUCTION

Hook (Larry's definition): A catchy memorable part of the song.

It might be the chorus, or a repeating "la, la, la, la, la." It might be the guitar riff at the beginning of "Layla" by Eric Clapton, or the repeating synthesizer riff of "Kids" by MGMT. It's the part of the song that once it gets in your ear, it is hard to get rid of it.

When I went to record this song in 2008, I had to look at the lyrics and consider just how much the technology had evolved. The original second verse lyrics went "Mommy and Daddy lend us their car, to go to the sold out show. We stand on our seats to get a glimpse, of the God we worship on our stereo."

By 2005 or 2006, the idea of a stereo record player was an antique notion. So, I had to change with the then times and say "Mommy and Daddy drop us off in the concert parking lot. We stand on our seats to get a glimpse of the God we worship, on our new iPods".

Now at this time the iPod is a quaint notion as most music comes through streaming services and apps on our cellphones. Vinyl and record players are actually making a comeback in many DJ and rock circles as people are reverting to the warmer and more dynamic analog sound. I wonder if by the time this book comes out, something new will have come to market and the replacement line will need to once again be replaced. You may say I'm a dreamer, but in my imagination, one day we will hear music telepathically outdating all physical devices.

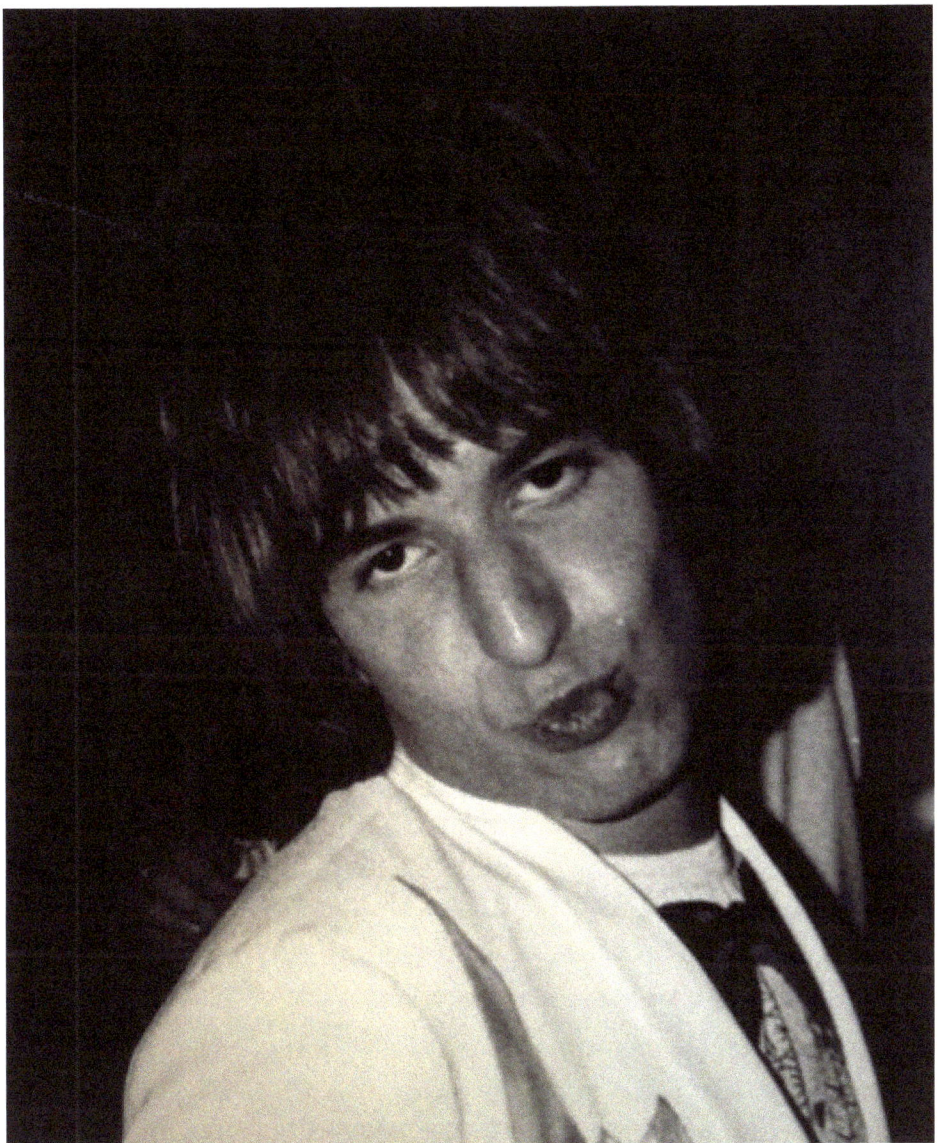
They say "youth is wasted on the young…" Who would argue?

But the point is the same. We love our favorite songs, and the music stars that sing them. They touch us deeply – emotionally, spiritually, even sexually. That will never change.

ENDING

I have always loved "Bohemian Rhapsody" by Queen. I'm not sure if I've ever met someone who didn't? Even the Muppets have done a YouTube version, and it's both a hilarious and brilliant parody. So after the second verse of "The King of Trite," I wanted to go into something wonderfully weird. A Dr. Zhivago type Russian melody. In my mind's eye I imagined dancing polar bears, and Cossacks drinking vodka in the snow. And the "La la la la" vocal part, which is played in unison by the electric guitar, came out of that early eighties thing that certain artists did. David Bowie sang in a rather macho, baritone register on "Let's Dance." Talking Heads front man David Byrne sang in a baritone voice, too. I simply wanted it to go somewhere unexpected. And musically perhaps, show off my classical keyboard training.

The slow down after the musical bridge, "He's the King of Trite the new sensation" with major 7th piano chords was what I call my Manilow moment. He was at the time, one of the most recognized adult contemporary artists. Being a born-and-bred rocker more into Led Zeppelin, Mr. Manilow symbolized for me as a rebellious and perhaps immature youth, the ultimate "The King of Trite." He wrote a few of his hits, but Clive Davis selected most.

Or, perhaps I was just jealous that Clive hadn't selected any of my songs at the time to be recorded?

Clive Davis admits throughout his autobiography *The Soundtrack of My Life* that he is a lawyer turned record president because of a series of falling upward lucky circumstances, and of course because of relentless hard work.

Yet he candidly admits that he has no musical abilities whatsoever – just an instinct for the tastes of the common man, coupled with a voracious competitive streak. He made Barry famous and most of the big hits came from the one or two songs per album that Clive was contractually allowed to select for Mr. Manilow. It was a transition moment in regards to the music business where a lawyer and corporate head selects the material for an artist to perform. As Joni Mitchell wrote in "Both Sides Now" that Judy Collins made famous: "Something's lost and something's gained, in living every day."

We're off to see the wizard! Clive has been a personal friend and mentor since 1979.

Back to "The King of Trite." The sound effects after the song ends and segues to the next are, for me, a favorite technique I picked up from Pink Floyd. Their albums are like a tapestry, a journey through a wormhole of time and space where songs are connected by sound effects, voices, synths, footsteps. I wanted the ending of "The King of Trite" to sound like a person changing stations in a car to find something they like…A jumble of words and sounds. Hidden away is a line from a Beatles song: "close your eyes and I'll kiss you, tomorrow I'll miss you." At the end of "All You Need Is Love" during the fade there is a moment when Paul sings, "she loves you yeah yeah yeah." I was simply recreating that in my own way.

Sir Paul, please don't sue me!

POP SECRET #2: BITTERSWEET LYRIC – HAPPY MUSIC

It's the contrast of colors that often makes a great piece of art – the white canvas against whatever color is painted onto its surface. It's this contrarian principle that holds true for many of music's greatest songs: bittersweet words, happy music!

Take for example "I'll Never Fall In Love Again" by Burt Bacharach and Hal David:

"What do you get when you fall in love, you only get lies, and pain, and sorrow, so for at least until tomorrow, I'll never fall in love again."

Or "Hallelujah" by Leonard Cohen:

"It's not a cry you hear at night, it's not somebody who's seen the light, it's a cold, and it's a broken Hallelujah."

Gosh, these wretched writers! How we listeners identify with them for writing something so emotionally dark about the shadowy side of love.

Yet both songs are juxtaposed against major sounding chords. The Burt Bacharach/Hal David song is so light and peppy it could be part of a soap commercial on television.

The opposite is true as well.

We can balance words that express a lot of sunshine by giving them a few musical "clouds." That way, our compositions don't feel so green on green, white on white, red on red, black on...black.

ANOTHER "BE AUDACIOUS" STORY

I believe that my audacity in 1983 to pick up my life and move to a city where I didn't speak, read or write the language, and didn't know anyone personally, quite possibly saved my life.

Having bottomed out in New York after failing to secure a record contract, I needed a break from the hamster wheel of city life. I was told Munich was a green city. That meant less urban, with more parks and nature. I was told people in Munich had a fondness for American musicians. I don't recall if I bothered to fact check if this were true, I just decided to take a leap of faith.

Before I left New York I asked everyone I knew for any introductions to mutual friends in Germany, either personal or professional. Like a musical immigrant, I arrived with a suitcase in one hand, a keyboard in the other.

At first, I stayed with a friend of a friend, then at a hotel. Several days after arriving I met a young English guy in a café who said he was a booking agent. Soon, he was my booking agent. Next, I met a band in a beer garden, and they offered to let me crash at their place. Soon I had a band. Then a record label – which my lawyer from New York had introduced me to offered me a record deal along with a full salary to live on, a recording studio facilities, and they even offered to find me an apartment.

Everything I had tried to get together and ultimately failed to find in New York came together during my first two weeks in Munich. I completely had let go, trusted, and followed my joy. I was not being realistic, and of course I threw caution to the wind being in the folly of my youth. In other words I was being Audacious!

Each day I'd go to the flat of some of my new friends and play an old out-of-tune upright piano. It was like a scene from a beat poet movie; this run-down European building, the many rooms with different roommates, and a crazed 23 year old American plunking away on the keys for hours. It was here that I started writing "Each One of Us."

When I moved to London in late 1984, the song came with me. When I moved back to New York in 1986, the song came along with me. I knew it was special in 1989 when I recorded a number of piano/vocal demos in Woodstock and "Each One of Us" stood out. It just popped its head out of the middle of forty other songs announcing, "Here I am, pay attention!"

The chilling part about my audacity to dive into the unknown by moving alone with no job to a foreign country and city, only dawned on me when I moved back to New York. By 1986 the city was ground zero for the spread of a new disease called AIDS. No one quite understood it yet, or how it was transmitted. The nightlife scene was decimated, people were afraid of shaking hands or even standing next to someone who sneezed.

I had moved from New York, to Munich, which was by comparison a very provincial city with far less risk , just at the moment AIDS first started to spread.

To repeat this again, I believe that my being audacious and what seemed crazy to some to just pick up my whole life and move to a city where I didn't speak, read or write the language, and didn't know anyone personally, helped save my life.

At the time of this writing I've received countless calls, emails, and messages from people touched by the spirit and sound of "Each One of Us." It has something timeless that I didn't intend, but I am very happy knowing that it reaches into people's minds and hearts. Is it the leaping acrobatic chorus melody? Is it the lyrics, asking the questions why am I here, what is the meaning of my life? That is the essence of much of what we're discussing in this book: writing something timeless, a blank canvas for each person to project their own meaning upon.

I always had an inclination for seeking enlightenment and spirituality, maybe not in the form of traditional religion, but in the form of a more esoteric and sublime personal pilgrimage. I'd read books, chanted with Buddhists, learned to meditate with Sufis, read the Bible, the Torah, the Koran. I even met a guy who said flying saucers would uncloak themselves from another dimension and communicate with him.

I had always had a vision in my head of the place we go after we die, kind of like a heavenly passport control. In my mind's eye I see an American Indian, next to a civil war solider, next to a holy prophet, next to tyrant, next to a king, next to a beggar, all the same in the end.

Without getting into the way each person brought good or bad upon himself, herself or the world, I saw each radiant soul reach the podium and have their passport stamped "HUMAN BEING."

The Mokes, Kailua Hawaii (January 2014)

This image that we are all destined to become equal parts of this greater whole often brings me to tears, even to this day.

The song offers the lesson that we often stoop so low to reach so high. Our lives are full of constant impermanent effort, striving, hopes, fears, pain and joy, sorrow and happiness: the full wheel of human experience. It's the same for each one of us.

So that is how the song "Each One of Us" began in Munich. The questions we ask ourselves again and again throughout time are "What's my purpose? Why am I here?"

The conclusion I've arrived at after all my searching and questioning seems to come back to the answer being within, that we are each a spark of the universe, a light upon an ocean of lights called creation.

EACH ONE OF US

Words and Music by: Larry Dvoskin

How many times have you asked why?
what's my purpose here in this life?
the longer I live
the more that I learn, we've just begun.
Some meditate in prayer, and burn incense
some fight 'for the right' with such pretense
we reach for the answer only to find, it's within us
Each One of Us
Each One of Us
Will find all the answers and be with the master
in time
Presidents and kings often fail
many have tried but few prevail
you can spin the cosmic wheel
but you cannot make her pay before her
Each One of Us
Each One of Us
Will find all the answers and be with the master
in time
Will find all the answers and become the master
in time.

THE SONG DECONSTRUCTION

There is a verse here that is missing. It's truly the best one of all but somehow ended up on the editing room floor, so to speak. It was meant to come after the bridge and tie it all together. It goes like this:

Each one of us will surely die
And cue up by the gate in the sky
As we go through passport control
They stamp your visa:
Human Being
Each One of Us
Will find all the answers
and become the master, in time.

MELODY

The whole chorus melody dances. In and out of the chord notes, a minor second here, a 4th there. It lifts the music up with both headline leaps and tension and release resolves. I did this intuitively. I wanted something to stand out, really make a musical statement that separated the chorus from the verses.

The word "Each" is an E note against G# minor chord. For those of you that scratch your head say "whaaa!?" – the chord has a D# note that is right next to an E, it's the black key below it, right next door. If you play a D3 and an E together, it sounds like a cat walking across the piano keyboard. It sounds harsh and dissonant.

Yet the "Each" is a tension note, actually an augmented note against the G# minor, followed by "one of," which sounds normal until the word and note of "us." It's a B note against an A chord. Again, a dissonant clash. The B note against the A is the same note as the first note in Paul McCartney's "Yesterday." In the key of F, the "Yea" is a G against an F chord… or a second. To give you a further description, in the do, re, mi, fa of a major scale, it's the re played at the same time as the do: "Clashy Poo!"

So, the word "each" is an augmented clash tension note, then the "us" is as well. During the next line the each is an F# note against a C# minor chord, a 4th, and another tension note. Then it resolves with a very headline-type acrobatic leap on "One of Us." As we discussed, this type of big dramatic melody leap can make a lasting, positive impression on the listener. The "us" at the end is a "G# against an A chord, another tension note but positioned to sound sweet as a major 7th. Then in the next line the word "find" is a 4th. A B note against an F sharp minor chord.

CHORDS

I used very happy-sounding major chords in the verse, minor sounding chords in the chorus to differentiate the sections, kinda like The Beatles "Help," and my own song "Brothers and Sisters." It goes from major to minor, which really gives the song a very distinct structure.

If there is anything I'm dissatisfied about with this song (besides everything, like most artists!) it's the bridge. I never found the inspiration to write anything more. I believe I tried to come up with something unique, but all I could come up with is this double time, Dr. Zhivago-type part. I had images of horses running through the snow pulling carriages filled with Russian royalty.

PRODUCTION

The track began with a freeform piano and vocal recording, no click or metronome. I wanted it to deliberately slow down and speed up in sections and feel "right" rather than be "correct."

Like many of the songs on the album, it had a long, winding birth. The first musicians I hired to worked on it – just couldn't deliver the music I was hearing in my head. One person made it sound like a Disney movie. Another made it sound hard rock and angry. It's not an angry song.

As mentioned I am influenced by Pink Floyd, so I wanted a softer, more psychedelic atmosphere like their song "Us and Them."

Finally, after it changed hands three or four times with each set of people I hired to program or play on it, somehow it just arrived at how it sounds today.

It needed a lot of reverb, and I believe from my conversation with the person who mixed it, there are at least four different delays on the lead vocal set at different rates, panned left/right so that it gives it that lofty, creamy effect.

The live string quartet really gave the song some emotional depth and instrument warmth. Much of production in this day and age is machines, so anytime a real human is playing, a real heart is felt. I hired young students from Manhattan School of Music to play, and I cut it live in my living room. As there are many different approaches toward music production, I am a big-picture type producer. I often describe myself as a "musical air traffic controller."

Over the years I've spent thousands of hours doing it. It becomes an instinct for each individual artist and song of knowing what the best studios and musicians are, what arrangement sounds best, the right key, tempo, etc. To cut this string section I did something very old school: I recorded the quartet live around a single microphone with the speakers on. The musicians weren't wearing headphones.

Of course the sound coming from the speakers bled into the mic, as did the other string players but this created a sound much like the overhead mics of a drum kit. Then I switched the speakers off and on headphones one by one recorded each individual instrument. This way they could play together as a quartet, yet I could also separate the violins, viola and cello parts on individual tracks for mixing. The combination worked out great.

Record your own notes here:

CHAPTER 4. SEE LIFE AS ENERGY

See life as energy, not a straight line. Surround yourself with people who bring you up, see the light in you and help to make you shine brighter.

Think of life as music on the radio. If you don't enjoy the song being played, switch stations. You will start to notice a change. It can be frightening. It ain't easy letting go of bad relationships, jobs, family members who radiate negativity. There is a saying that rings true: "Negative people see a problem in every solution."

"I know for sure that what we dwell on is who we become." – Oprah Winfrey

MY "SEE LIFE AS ENERGY" STORY

I read the book *Under the Tuscan Sun* in 1998. The story is about a housewife from California who moves to Italy during a midlife crisis and to renovate an old farmhouse. She becomes a new person amid the challenges of living in a foreign land, and gains a whole new perspective about her future. She finds magic in the sunlight streaming through curtains and the way flowers seemed to nod their "heads" in the breeze.

While reading this book I had a dream about her farmhouse where I found shooting stars under her dining room table. Of course, this would be impossible in physical terms, but to me it represented finding magic in the mundane, mixing two worlds that don't normally exist together.

Songwriters consciously or not, often try to write the song they wished they had written by someone else. I set about writing "It's

The End of the World as We Know It (And I Feel Fine)" by REM. I just loved the splatter of words thrown at the listener during the verse, and the smooth melody of the chorus that provides contrast. It felt to me when first hearing this song that the age of information overload was perfectly represented by the spew of verse images, and the "whatever" attitude of the chorus lyric.

Fields of Gold, Tuscany Italy

These two inspirations – the colorful magic in the mundane imagery of *Under the Tuscan Sun*, mixed with a list of stream-of-consciousness verse lyrics – inspired me to write "Love Heels." The title is spelled correctly. It's about how true love is both a force of creation and destruction all at once: birth and death. Therefore it humbles us, breaks us down, refines us, and then lifts us up into the sunlight for all the world to see.

In 1998, I was in an expansion phase. I was in love and living with the person of my dreams. In addition I had a multi-million selling album out with songs I had co-written on it. I was traveling a lot, "moving on up," as they say. Much like they say that the rich get richer, so too does good lead to better when we SEE LIFE AS ENERGY. Just focus on the good, and the good increases; focus on what you lack and it increases, too. It's the law of physics. Of course it's easier to focus on the good when the good times are rolling. The challenge is to be able to be grateful and stay positive even in the midst of hard times.

LOVE HEELS

Words and Music by: Larry Dvoskin

At night there are stars under my table
the knife that I feared might stab me in the back
just cut loose the chord that bound me in misunderstanding
and helped me see a bigger picture
we are part of something greater, something deeper,
something wider, something harsher and now…
Love Heels, love breaks my illusions
Love steals, love fakes like a pauper at my table
Love Heels, love breaks like a barrel on the north shore
Love Heels, love breaks…
I've always been an underdog, never the popular one who
fits into the cool crowd, like a hand in a smooth lambskin glove
I am reaching for the sun but clouds pull like curtains
to drape me in shadows, and I'm ready for a new paradigm
a tableau, a stage right curtain call.
Love Heels, love breaks my illusions
Love steals, love fakes like a pauper at my table
Love Heels, love breaks like a barrel on the north shore
Love Heels, love breaks…
down every wall, it breaks the speed of sound
it brought me to my knees.
I woke up this morning head in a cloud
had a cup of coffee and a look out into
a new year new day new coat of paint
I entered the tunnel of pleasure and pain
the lesson and the teachin' of the story told that
to hold on I had to let go, of your love that I tied to me

like an eagle I had to set it free.
Love Heels, love breaks my illusions
Love steals, love fakes like a pauper at my table
Love Heels, love breaks like a barrel on the north shore
Love Heels, love breaks...
At night there are stars under my table

THE SONG DECONSTRUCTION

Like the hand holding a dog on a leash, love pulls at us to heel, as much as it pulls us to heal. It lifts us up and crashes down "like a barrel on the north shore," which refers to a surfing term used in Hawaii. The North Shore is where the best waves are on the island of Oahu, and the barrel is the obvious image of the curve of the wave that surfers aim toward riding inside of as long as possible until the wave unravels.

The Bonzai Pipeline, Oahu Hawaii (2014)

I think some of the chorus lyric was an unintended jab at a lover I had at the time – someone I was really taking care of, supporting, mentoring. When we fall deep in love, the small stuff doesn't matter, or it shouldn't. **All we take away from life in the end is the experience, memories, and the people we've loved.**

For a while I was using the word silhouette quite often. Then, I used translucent for a while. In this song I was proud of myself for pulling off the use of the word *paradigm*, as well as *tableau*. These words are rare for a pop song.

The second verse is the most autobiographical. I was like the ugly duckling that became a swan. Music gifted me silken wings.

I went from nerdy un-athletic kid in middle school, to being in the coolest band in town by high school. So the lyric "I've always been an underdog, never the popular one who fits into the cool crowd" is about myself. The "lambskin glove" is the type of winter gloves I was wearing at the time. The "reaching for the sun" line is the human impulse to strive, to reach, to grow, to have our time in the sun.

The bridge lyric was inspired by New Year's Eve 1999. I woke up hung over on January 1st with a "head in a cloud, had a cup of coffee and a look out into a new year, new day, new coat of paint." This refers to it actually being New Year's Day, and we were painting my apartment so it had the smell and texture of new paint in the air. The "tunnel of pleasure and pain" refers to a nightclub which we went to on New Year's Eve, but left almost immediately as the music was too loud, the place was too over crowded, and the vibe terrible. Yet, outside there was a line around the block of pleasure-seeking lotus eaters, eager to get in.

My partner at that time reacted very strongly to the line "to hold on I had to let go of your love." I had to make assurances that I wasn't thinking of breaking up, but rather simply setting up the line about the eagle, the national symbol of American freedom. For the line "like an eagle I had to set it free" I was doing what composers sometimes do to amuse myself with an inside joke for only myself. A friend at Sony Records was working with the performer known as Eagle-Eye Cherry at that time, so I wanted to see if I could fit that artists name into the song lyric.

I have always liked books or films that end back at the beginning. Like *The Wizard of Oz*, when Dorothy awakens to find it was all a dream, yet each person she took for granted back in Kansas, was a powerful friend she met in Oz. So I liked the cliffhanger feeling of starting and ending on "at night there are stars under my table."

MELODY

This is why music, the songwriting rabbit in particular, is such an elusive "hare" to spot and track down. For every rule we apply, there is a glowing example which becomes successful that has broken it. Nothing rhymes in the verses, it's not an even number of measures (usual verses are 8 measures, a 4 measure pre chorus, 8 measure chorus, etc.).

Without infringing on anyone's work, I took inspiration from "It's the End of the World as We Know It" and created a simple, very bold headline-type chorus melody to offset the stream-of-consciousness verse.

What's great about this song is I can sing and play it on a guitar and it sounds complete. I don't need the other instruments for it to come to life, but with the production it comes to life fully orchestrated as well.

CHORDS AND ARRANGEMENT

It's the simplest pattern: G, D, A minor, C for most of the song.

It's almost the famous 1, minor six, four, five pattern, but I substitute minor 2nd (A minor) instead. So the chord pattern for most of the song is 1, 5, minor 2, 4.

We break into a reggae beat in the bridge just to change things up a bit, and the melody follows with a more sharp tack like staccato feel, to differentiate from the more spoken rap feel of the verse.

PRODUCTION

This is another example of something I teach in my songwriting courses. Just like the first song "Life Is Strange," sometimes you just have to keep recording and rerecording until you get it right. I released a different version of this track on my first solo effort "Beside Me," which is a collection of demos. I must have recorded and rerecorded at least five different versions of "Love Heels," each time getting close to what I was imagining in my mind's eye, yet missing the mark. Each time I had to pay a whole new set of musicians, studios, and mix engineers to create a new version. The listener doesn't know that. The listener only knows whether it touches them or not. I finally reached a version I felt happy with, the one on "Life Is Strange".

ANOTHER "SEE LIFE AS ENERGY" STORY

In 2008 I attended a fundraiser for Hillary Clinton at a small intimate gathering in East Hampton, New York. At the last minute Mrs. Clinton couldn't make it, so her husband stepped in, former President Bill Clinton. I paid a modest donation and was treated to a very warm speech and Q&A afterward with only fifty people and Mr. Clinton. At one time a few years after he left the White House, there was a poll conducted worldwide in about one hundred countries asking, "Who is the most popular living human being today?"

The winner of this poll? William Jefferson Clinton

I could see why. He could answer almost any question about anything with lightning speed and razor-sharp clarity, like a supercomputer. Someone asked about U.S. relations with China, and he pulled up a paragraph from some piece of legislation from 1972 that no one had ever heard of and quoted a line from page one thousand something.

Regardless of your political affiliation, as a person he just was and still is as of the first edition of this book, amongst the race of super humans.

The next day I woke up still feeling the mojo from being in the presence of a person who some have named the most well-liked person on the planet, and went to a morning yoga class across from where I was staying in Amagansett, New York. I was in a hand stand when I looked across to see a face peering through the window. The window was a series of smaller squares and all I could see was a nose and eyes. But that nose and eyes looked improbably like Paul McCartney's. I thought to myself, "That's impossible. Why would Sir Paul be peering through the window of my yoga class like some peeping Tom?" It didn't make sense.

After yoga I went outside and behind the studio was a vegetarian sandwich shop. Sitting alone at a picnic table, there he was, the man himself and alone unguarded: Paul McCartney. He looked up at me and smiled, and before I could even think about it I approached him and said something like "Hi, I'm Larry, a songwriter who has been deeply inspired by your songs. I actually teach songwriting and use your song 'Yesterday' as an example of tension and release in melody." He was warm and friendly and asked how? I explained, "The first melody note was a G, against an F chord. This creates a tension aurally, a conflict. The 'Yes' of the word was a G rubbing against an F, and then the 'terday' was an F note upon the F chord, providing the release.

He looked at me like he had never thought about this technical detail before, and he genuinely appeared to be fascinated. He invited me to sit down. Now picture the scene:

Me, a child when Paul McCartney was the most famous rock star on Earth, and me now, a strange man to him soaked in perspiration and dressed only in shorts, tank top and carrying nothing. No wallet, phone, nada, singing away at him.

We sat there talking for about an hour. I had the extreme pleasure of asking Paul every question that had ever crossed my mind about the Beatles, the songs, his life.

I went on at first explaining what my tension and release theory was based on. For instance the "why" lyric from the middle 8 section is an A note, against an E minor chord. This is a weird thing, trust me! It's actually harder to sing when you deconstruct it. I found myself sitting across from him singing. In moments I thought to myself "Why are you singing at Paul McCartney!? He's the most famous singer on Earth!!! Shut up!" I was always the guy who had the microphone taken away from him in bands growing up because I'd sing really off pitch. Either by ignorance, arrogance, experience or some combination of all three, I've come a long way.

Paul was very friendly and inquisitive. We talked about songs, life, quantum physics, the Clintons, fame, my life, and his own.

At one point I asked him point-blank if the song "Hey Jude" was really about "Hey John?" I mean, wasn't it John who would take a sad song and make it better? Or, carry the world upon his shoulders?

Paul insisted it was about Julian Lennon. Originally "Hey Jules." Paul didn't like the ending of the word Jules, so he changed it by dropping the "s" to Jude, a more definitive end sound. He also told me that when he first played the song for John and Yoko he told them that he would rewrite the lyric "The movement you need is on your shoulder." John disagreed. He said it was his favorite line in the whole song and not to change it.

We talked about the Clintons, whom Paul had met many times and knew well. I mentioned how meeting Bill was like taking some kind of energy drink. Long after the handshake there is a buzz, which in my case lasted for weeks. I hypothesized with Paul that quantum physics is the new psychedelia … that science today, with quarks, sub-atomic particles, string theory and parallel universes, is doing what Dr. Timothy Leary was doing in the 1960s … that meeting someone who influenced the world like Bill Clinton has, would change the vibrational frequency of the people standing next to him. Think of the saying, "You are the company you keep."

Paul seemed to make a connection in his mind at this point. He explained that he started a school in Liverpool, and that he felt that just being in the room with the students, was somehow helpful. I chimed in that indeed it was his vibrational frequency that would lift up the frequency of everyone in the room.

It wasn't a cosmic "woo-woo" thing. It was scientific fact. This, according to Paul that day at the picnic table, was an "a-ha" moment.

He also went on to tell me about how he used to love watching the Carl Sagan stuff about space and the idea that we are literally "made up of the stars." Matter from the birth of stars eons ago has been floating around the universe and some of it is embedded into our DNA. Some of the molecules that made up the saber-tooth tiger are also floating around and part of our cells.

People came and went. Paul got the vegetarian dosa he ordered, and I ordered and ate one too. A few people stared but no one interrupted our chat. This was the Hamptons, where billionaires and stars are everywhere, so people are on their best behavior, even at 11:00 AM, on a sunny July morning.

After a while, I started to feel it was time to go. I just stood up, shook his hand and said something casual like, "See you again sometime." I had no pen for an autograph, no camera for a picture. It was just an out-of-the-blue conversation, a meeting of two men to discuss melody, friends, quantum physics, and life.

A few years later I'd meet him again, backstage at the 2012 Grammy awards. I was with the Beach Boys during a dress rehearsal during the morning of the show. We were called to sound check, and Paul was hanging out in the hallway backstage.

When he saw Brian, Mike, Alan he freaked out like a music fan and stopped them to say hello and take photos. Since cameras were forbidden backstage before the televised event to prevent the evenings Grammy broadcast from being leaked online, I of course broke the rules and whipped out my camera phone. I started snapping pictures of the Beatle meeting the Beach Boys.

Then Paul turned to me and asked if I wanted a picture, too. After my Hamptons experience, I never thought I'd have the opportunity again. It was such a mad, crazy moment with people crowding around and handlers trying to move in and safe guard Paul that I forgot to mention that summer lunch in The Hamptons we shared two years earlier. Instead as we stood side by side for the picture he put his arm on my shoulder, pointed to me and whispered in my ear "Ya know, this is gonna cost you 50 quid. I am Paul McCartney, ya know?"

My camera wouldn't work! It was somehow set to video, and wouldn't take a photo. The person I handed it to struggled to figure it out. Paul's handlers pressed in to snatch him, as other people thronged for photos too. As with all world-famous living legends, it was hot under the spotlight next to him. So what did Paul do?

Listen to what the man says: Sir Paul McCartney and I backstage at *The 2012 Grammy Awards*

He leaned in again and said "Ya know, I'm Paul McCartney and if I have to wait it's gonna cost you 100 quid." He just seemed to be in the happiest, light, playful mood and was clearly *taking the piss*, which is an English expression for playing a practical joke on someone. Finally we got the picture and away he went, leaving me with a remarkable "Life Is Larry" story.

Back to "Brothers and Sisters." After lunch with Paul, I rushed back to the place I was staying and started writing the song. I was staying with a friend who sings and writes country music. In one of the songs he sang and recorded, there was a single line at the ending of a song called "Stick It to the Man." During the last chorus he casually improvised "brothers and sisters, stick it to the man." That morning I woke up hearing "brothers and sisters" in my head and wrote the chorus. You know how dreams are, they don't have to make sense. This line was so random and small. It played in my head and the chorus came out in a dream and I rushed to write it down before yoga.

Then "Paul" happened. I wrote the rest of the lyric based on our conversation.

BROTHERS AND SISTERS
Words and Music by: Larry Dvoskin

Met a man who told me 'let it be'
He'd lost everything but somehow was at peace
Met a girl, who sold her soul to gain the world
But it didn't bring her happiness the diamonds or the pearls
Brothers and Sisters – the time has come
Brothers and Sisters – together we are one
Brothers and Sisters – it's just you and me
Around the World – All around the world
Met a child building castles in the sand
We stoop so low at times and still don't understand
The moment's now – right across your shoulder
Don't look back don't look ahead
Don't wait until you're older
Sisters – the time has come
Brothers and Sisters – together we are one
Brothers and Sisters – got to be free
Around the World – All around the world

Love love love
A moment of silence between you and I
There's a force within once it begins, that cannot be denied
You and I are made up of the stars
We are truly one now, in matter and in heart
Brothers and Sisters – All around the world

THE SONG DECONSTRUCTION

The first two lines are about Paul. As we spoke I marveled about how the general public only sees the super-wealthy, famous rock star Paul, yet privately he endured more personal loss than many people. First, his mother died when he was young, then he tragically lost his manager Brian Epstein without whom the world would have never known about the Beatles.

Without Mr. Epstein who knows, Paul might be driving a truck or something? Then he lost John, his dearest friend, songwriting partner, and creative competitor. Then he lost Linda, mother to some of his children and longest lasting love of his life. Many people would have turned to drugs or ended their own life. Not Paul. He simply got busy touring, writing, and recording new songs, and along the way becoming vegan.

The second two lines "met a girl who sold her soul to gain the world, but it didn't bring her happiness the diamonds or the pearls" was about a pushy, self-entitled woman at the Clinton fundraiser. This very rich looking, bejeweled Southampton "princess" was enraged that the Secret Service agents assigned to accompany Mr. Clinton asked her to enter through a garage entrance into the house where he was, instead of through the front door. She reacted as if it were the greatest of insults and argued with them about which door she was willing to walk through. To me, it was a tiny house and the other door was just a few yards away. She was apparently someone who felt superior to others even when in the presence of a president of the United States. I thought to myself, "This woman has everything materially, but she must be a miserable person."

She was ready to leave the event because she wasn't allowed to roam freely as she wanted, and she just couldn't let it go. So the first part of the first verse is about Paul losing his most cherished people and forging ahead, and second part of the same verse is about a spoiled rich woman who felt entitled to cause a major drama over nothing of consequence.

The second verse was simply that I went to Indian Wells Beach in Amagansett, and there was a sand castle competition. The whole beach was a delightful construction site of castles with moats, towers, pyramids, and temples. So I wrote about man and woman in verse one, and then about a child in verse two. I've always loved the saying *we stoop so low to reach so high*, so I included that, too. Then I circled back to my Paul conversation and included the line he was going to change in "Hey Jude," "The movement you need is on your shoulder." I like the "do it now" message of "don't look back, don't look ahead, don't wait until you're older."

The last verse again relates to my conversation with Paul. He told me that so often during the Beatles and Wings touring days, he'd play in these huge stadiums and the lights shining on him were so bright he never really got to see the audience. He told me that in recent years he decided to stop playing at some point in the show, turn the house lights on in the audience, and just quietly look back at all the people. They were looking at him, so why couldn't he take a few moments to look back?

So the line "a moment of silence between you and I" relates to Paul's moment during each concert when he pauses.

And as mentioned before "you and I are made up of the stars" is what he quoted Carl Sagan as saying.

CHORDS

Often throughout this book, I'll repeat a concept or state an idea more than once so it really sinks in with the reader and takes root. As we discussed previously in the Pop Secret of 1, minor 6, 4, 5, this is the oldest trick in the book. These chords in any order or variation are hardwired to the brain, telling our neuro-receptors to open sesame.

Why? Again, here's my own non-scientific, completely wild guess take on it. We've all seen the nature shows where one animal lets out a sound, and the whole flock runs for safety. Soon after, a lurking predator makes itself known, prowling to strike a kill.

The human brain has evolved similarly through time to be wary of anything foreign or unknown (a possible snake or tiger in the bushes) and open to what we know, trust, and is familiar. This applies to sounds as well.

So we hear G, E minor, C, D, and somewhere deep in the recesses of our minds there floats the warm familiar sound of "Stand by me, woah stand by me," or "Every breath you take, every move you make, every bond you break, every step you take I'll be watching you," or even, "Baby baby baby oh, baby baby baby oh, baby baby baby ohh, I thought you'd always be mine."

What do Ben E. King, The Police, and Justin Bieber all have in common?

1, minor 6, 4 5, hardwired to the open receptors in our brain.

I didn't intentionally sit down and say to myself, "Oh, I wanna write a song people will immediately be receptive to, by opening neural pathways, so I will use these chords." It was a simple spur-of-the moment intuitive process.

The verse chords of "Brothers and Sisters" are slightly switched around as G, D, E minor, C = 1, 5, minor 6, 4. Then the same chords pattern gets switched around again in the chorus E minor, C, D = minor 6, 4, 5. If you compare them, you may notice that in the verse of "Brothers and Sisters" it is the same pattern as "With or Without You" by U2. Did "Brothers and Sisters" sound like U2 on first listen? Chances are the answer is no.

ARRANGEMENT

Because the verse is based around the G chord and is very major sounding, I based the chorus around the E minor, so it goes from major to minor and clearly makes a sonic distinction between sections.

This is what the Beatles did in "Help." The verse is based on a major chord G, then the chorus a minor chord= A minor.

The chorus chords for "Brothers and Sisters" are also similar to "Heart of Gold" by Neil Young and many other songs. E minor, C, D. It just moves differently, with a very different melody, structure, and beat.

To change it up, the bridge section also starts on the minor chord, E minor, with simple full harmonies over the chords that are very much sustained. This adds contrast to the melody of the verse and chorus, which is very rhythmic, and in places staccato.

PRODUCTION

At a festival named Burningman, which I attended in 2010, friends and I saw and hoped onboard a Magic Carpet art car.

No I wasn't dreaming. It was a real motorized vehicle someone built by stripping down a golf cart and refurbishing it. On it were a variety of African instruments and in my mind I heard this doumbek-drum type of beat, a world beat feeling I had on this magic carpet ride. As with much of art, when it came time to produce "Brothers and Sisters," it didn't fully turn out as I had envisioned in my mind's eye, and I'd probably still be working on it today if left to my own perfectionism. I heard this song as a global type of thing, a peace song.

I always think about how different we are in each part of the world, and how often color, sex, religion, nationality separate us from one another. Yet we have these simple words in common across each language. Mother, father, sister, brother.

I think about how we bond over such similarities and are really all the same.

That is why despite the song being, in my opinion the most under produced on the album, I let it go. Just like John Lennon's "Imagine," in my own imagination as a producer, it could be a million times better, but its simplicity is its magic.

POP SECRET #3: START WITH A SPECTACULAR FIRST LINE

My friend Victoria Shaw co-wrote "The River" for Garth Brooks, and helped discover and produce country super group Lady Antebellum. She said to me that often during writing sessions in Nashville, rather than coming in with a great song title, or chorus, she'll come in with a catchy first line of lyric.

My friend Jason Flom has worked as President/CEO at a number of major record labels from his own Lava imprint, to Capitol, Virgin, Atlantic, and Warner Brothers. He also told me that he often listens for a great first lyric line and that is the hook that grabs his attention. He told me the first song he heard by Matchbox Twenty, a band he signed, had a compelling first line and he was "in." He went to see his boss at the time and declared, "I'm signing this band!"

So if it works for them, it's worth considering for your own songs. Look at your first lines. Are they well-written, authentic, heartfelt, provocative?

Here are some first lines from songs on "Life Is Strange",

"Life Is Strange"
"The nipsy gypsy thought it was hip, she abandoned ship, she couldn't swim."
"Everyone's a Hooker"
"All my friends are hookers, drug addicts good lookers."
"King of Trite"
"He's the Wednesday is Sunday of songwriting singers, buy one get one free."
"Love Heels"
"At night there are stars under my table."

FIRST LINE DECONSTRUCTIONS

"Life Is Strange:" This is a play on words and rhyme schemes. Similar to "Being for the Benefit of Mr. Kite" by the Beatles: Kite, tonite, trampoline, there, faire, scene. The first two lines of "Mr. Kite" have an internal rhyme and the third and 6th line rhyme: trampoline and scene.

With "Life Is Strange" nipsy and gypsy rhyme along with hip and ship and swim rhymes with the last word of second line Jim. Its lyric imagery is intended to drive home the point that life is strange, indeed.

"Everyone's a Hooker," "All my friends are hookers, drug addicts good lookers." It works because the melody is a major 7th chord and note that you might hear in some very syrupy pop song, so juxtaposed against such harsh, revealing lyrics it sets up the song perfectly. And with the recording of a sweet girl's voice it also counter balances the darkness of the words if taken literally, with a lightness of chords and melody.

Record your own notes here:

CHAPTER 5. TRAVEL

For most of my adult life I have lived in New York City. Despite this I am often accused of traveling too much, being on permanent vacation, perhaps even living too well! My goodness!

I ask you the reader, "Do you live to work, or work to live?"

Don't let this man drink and drive! Captain's Seat of a Boeing 777, 2014

I am of the belief in the old Mae West quote: "Too much of a good thing is wonderful!" I travel, fill myself with good energy, colors, sights, sounds, smells, stars, nature, friends, dreams, music, and then I have a full tank of good energy to share with the people I work with. I have good vibes, and the work comes out better, easier, faster.

This is different from some Peter Pan escapism. It's actually alchemy. Getting in tune with the right frequency, the right mode to be my best, and therefore, to be the best person I can be toward loved ones, friends, family, and co-workers.

Ever notice the mood of people leaving on a plane for vacation? They are usually cranky, impatient, and tired-looking on the flight out. Ever notice the mood of the same planeload of people on the flight back? They are so much more relaxed, calmer even with loud babies crying in the next row. Which group of people would you rather work with or be around?

MY "TRAVEL" STORY

I was having a grand old time on the tropical island of Kauai in Hawaii with a group of friends during Thanksgiving in 2009. We were partying, going to the beach, just having the time of our lives. When my friends left to fly back home, I stayed in Hawaii, moving into a hotel on Hanalei beach. I knew about this tiny seaside town from the song I sang as a child, "Puff, The Magic Dragon." In addition to the obvious drug references, there was a mountain range which according to local folklore resembled the back of a dragon.

Perhaps with a bit more "puffing" I might have seen the dragon, too, but to me it just looked like every other bumpy mountain ridge.

I had everything: time, money, a great place, a great car, everything except the person I was dating at the time. They were back in NYC working, and it seemed they never actually had time to be in a relationship. I felt like my side of the relationship was something sacred, a potential soul mate "rest of my life for better or worse" thing, and for them, it was an item on a check list.

TO GET CHECKLIST

- Milk
- Eggs
- Almost-famous boyfriend

- Toilet Paper
- Almonds

Hanalei sunset – The Dragon's Back

You get the idea. So, composers often want to write the song they wish they'd written so as to emulate their heroes. I sat down feeling incomplete in this tropical paradise without someone to share it with.
I employed that sly old Pop Trick 101: bittersweet words and happy music or melody.

I was trying to write my Bruce Springsteen-sounding song. It came out different than anything I'd ever written, and I liked the application of a raspy vocal performance.

Needless to say, it was one of the last songs to be written and included on the album, and its legacy lives on far longer than that relationship which lasted only a couple of months.

The boss and I. Backstage Carnegie Hall New York City (April 5, 2007)

THE ONLY THING MISSING
Words and Music by: Larry Dvoskin

I got some cash, I got the car, I got the keys,
I got the hotel room with the perfect view
I got the waves, I got the sun, I got the surf,
I got the sand, I got my tan that much is true
Something is missing here in paradise
'Cause I got nothing without you right here by my side
The Only Thing Missing Is You
The Only Thing Missing,
That's breaking my little heart in two
And It's you, it's you, it's you, it's you

The Only Thing Missing – Is You
Ain't got a cold, ain't got a flat
Ain't got a worry – how 'bout that?
There ain't a cloud in the sky so blue
Ain't had a fight, ain't lost my job,
Ain't got no pain, I ain't been robbed
Except of sharing this paradise now with you
I got a feeling that excites me now
It's dreaming that you'll be here with me, any second now
The Only Thing Missing Is You
The Only Thing Missing,
That's breaking my little heart in two
And It's you, it's you, it's you, it's you
The Only Thing Missing – Is You

THE SONG DECONSTRUCTION

The first verse lists all the things the composer has. The second verse lists all the things the composer doesn't have. It's a more causal style than some of the other lyrics, the "I got this, I got that, ain't got this, ain't got that"…More like a Mick Jagger or Bruce Springsteen conversational lyric.

My favorite lyric here is the 5th and 6th lines of verse two. The fact that "Ain't got no pain, I ain't been robbed except of sharing this paradise now with you." I really like the flow of how the idea of being robbed plays in both directions and dimensions of an emotional as well as physical expression.

As mentioned in the chapter "The King of Trite" I was around Foreigner through our mutual manager, and their songs were the perfect blend of art and commerce for that era. Many of their hit songs had this uplifting message with lines like "I would climb any mountain, sail across a stormy sea," or "it must be the woman in you, that brings out the man in me."

And so I think this influenced me in writing the suddenly and perhaps unrealistically hopeful second B verse:

"I got a feeling that excites me now
It's dreaming that you'll be here with me, any second now"
Wishful thinking!

MELODY

Melodically, it's more rhythmical, and the rhythm of it drives the groove of the song. There is not much tension and release or dramatic headline leaps in the melody against the chords, but that creates the foundation for lots of vocal harmony layers. The tension notes melodically in the chorus dance between the chords.

CHORDS AND ARRANGEMENT

This is a very major chord, happy, American radio-type song. The music offsets the loneliness of the lyric. For those of you near an instrument, pick it up.

Pluck, play, strum G / C / D

That is the chorus. Now imagine if the chords were minor?

G minor, C minor, and to be consistent with often used chord patterns, D major.

It sounds like a totally different song. A vastly different mood, tonal colors beneath the lyric "The only thing missing is you."

Again, to make it an almost a sleight-of-hand magic trick, I use the major chords to offset the longing feeling of the lyric, so that the contrast is not like white on white.

The word "paradise" in the B-verse before the chorus, is outside the D major chord. It's a B note on the front half of the word "para," and then resolves with end of the word "paradise…" Then in the part just before the chorus…"right here by my side" is outside the D major chord with the word "right," an E note, then inside the chord with the note of D on "here", then the words "my side" are again outside the chord, a B note, until it resolves at the end of the word "side" on an A note.

The chorus also follows an easy melody, except the "It's you" part half way through, where it creates the pattern of tension and release again. Against a G chord you have an E note on the word "It's," and a D note outside of a C chord. Then you have an E note inside the chord of C, but a D on the "you" creating a 2nd or major 9th.

Sound confusing? Eventually I'll have an audio and video so you can hear the points being explained. You can also pick up a copy of the "Life Is Strange" album online to hear for yourself the deconstruction mentioned throughout this book. For now just know it's like the film *Star Wars*: A push and pull between opposing forces. It is this contrast that creates a compelling melody.

POP SECRET #4: LIST SONGS

A lot of hit song lyrics are comprised of lists. A whole barrage of words that point to a particular subject as exemplified in "The Only Thing Missing." An example of this is John and Yoko Ono Lennon's "Give Peace a Chance." In a very artful way, he talks about the million-and-one causes, and points of view, to make the point that in the end the answer to most of the problems in the world is a simple one: Give peace a chance.

The song doesn't have to preach. The point of so many opposing points of view does the preaching for us to enable us to see the absurd.

ANOTHER "TRAVEL" STORY

Several years before writing "The Only Thing Missing" I was on Maui, which for those who are unfamiliar with this state is a different island of Hawaii. Camping at a beachside state park I met an unusual hippie boy one day who it turns out was born in a cave there to hippie parents. They named him after a gorilla from a TV cartoon show, Magilla.

We became friends and, as he had studied therapeutic massage at school, I got a foot massage before bed. Asleep that night with the crash of the Pacific Ocean waves echoing through my dreams, I heard this song. I woke up and sang it into a tape recorder.

Reflexology is the art of foot massage. Not the usual topic for a songwriter! Even the word is technical, scientific. But there it was. I imagined the beat to be a very rhythmic jam that you might play around a campfire while banging on hand drums.

This song is truly old school in the sense it can be played with just a voice and guitar for a complete experience. Many classic songs are like this. The production is an added bonus.

I wanted a groovy world beat production a la Michael Franti, Bob Marley, but not purely reggae. As mentioned previously yet again it sometimes takes several tries recording a song before you hit gold. In this case I handed the song to several different programmer friends until it seemed to land in the right place.

REFLEXOLOGY

Words and Music by Larry Dvoskin

Reflexology, together in the night when the moon kicks off no light
No apology, for a passion I can't tame and a shakti I can't name
As I see strange things, and I dream strange dreams
Tina Turner is mad at me
Reflexology, awaken to the roar – opening the door
Wrapping all around me,
with a passion I can't tame and a shakti I can't name
I miss ring-a-ring, I go golden light bathing
It's for God alone, I sing
Wai napa napa napa napa napa napa
Baba, ba ba ba ba ba ba
Babaji
She's a boy and he's a girl, who renounced this world
It's the gorilla of my dreams
Reflexology, Reflexology

THE SONG DECONSTRUCTION

These lyrics will never win the Nobel Prize for great literature, but the song is musically different than anything else on the album. "Reflexology" is simple, yet twists and turns in unexpected ways. And it's meant to be softly whimsical.

She's a boy and he's a girl, who renounced this world

It's the gorilla of my dreams

My friend Magilla had very feminine features and waist-long blond hair. Many people mistook him for a woman even though he wasn't. He loved women and I'd joke with him about being a lesbian trapped in a man's body. The lyrics above reflect the Yin and Yang in each of us. We are composed of the DNA from both our mother and father.

The idea of "it's for God alone I sing" is the image of being alone in my park cabin, guitar in hand, singing to the sea and sky, sharing with God my solitary song.

The line "Tina Turner is mad at me" also came from the dream.

In this dream I was in a restaurant, and Tina Turner was there. I approached her table with a tape of a song to pitch to her. Needless to say, when I interrupted her meal, she got very angry at me. That's where this random line comes from.

MELODY

The melody isn't particularly noteworthy (no pun intended) in regard to tension and release or headline leaps. However, the part where I break up the words Wainapanapa and Babaji are sung very rhythmically and this creates its own hook. Like the song "No Scrubs" by TLC, sometimes a less evolved melody can be a great hook due to the groove the words create. The fast staccato in "Reflexology" is what makes this song stand apart from anything else on "Life Is Strange". To separate the verse from the middle eight part melodically, I do the opposite using long-held legato notes.

CHORDS

To separate the sections the song cycles between minor and major chords. The verse a fast A minor to E minor, giving it the gypsy-like campfire feel. Then the middle 8 or bridge sections are very major chord sounding from F major 7th, to C major 7th, ending on a G major with sustained melody notes. This keeps the song from becoming too repetitive.

Record your own notes here:

_____
_____
_____
_____
_____
_____
_____
_____
_____
_____
_____
_____
_____
_____
_____
_____
_____
_____

CHAPTER 6. BE OF SERVICE

The myth of capitalism is that the person with the most toys wins. Yet when we focus on the richest people who truly have it all, the only thing left once they've climbed to the mountain top is to help others up the mountain, too. To be of service.

As many readers may know, one of the richest men in the world at the time of this writing is Bill Gates. Mr. Gates retired from Microsoft to spend the rest of his life giving away his money to help others. One of the other richest men, Warren Buffett, joined forces to give much of his money to the Bill and Melinda Gates Foundation to also help save the world.

From Bono to Bill, billionaires like these more than ever at any time in history could sit in their mansions set for life. But with the world facing so many problems today, and governments and big corporations able to only provide part of the solution, people like Mr. Gates, Mr. Buffett, Bono and many others spend a good deal of their money, time, and energy trying to make the world a better place and lift up those less fortunate.

The Dali Lama is quoted as saying, "The happiest person is he who brings the most happiness to others." It's human nature to want something more: a better job, a career, a family, and more money. But just like the new Christmas toy whose luster soon fades after a short time, one of the ways to find true lasting happiness is to be of service to others. It's something in human makeup that brings a deeper, more lasting fulfillment than *what's in it for me*?

Being of service means more than just writing a check. Assets are multidimensional. For some it's money, for others it's ideas, time, volunteer work, social currency ("who you know"), or simply being there for a friend. The ways to be of service are varied, and we can each do something great or small each day to make a difference.

MY "BE OF SERVICE" STORY

"Journey through Life" is the only song I didn't write on my solo album "Life Is Strange". It was written in 1974 by my high school band mates Steve Lozowski and Jeff Lee.

The first big break in my music career was being hired in 1972 to play keyboards in Sunrise, a local cover band that played the songs of Chicago, Blood Sweat and Tears, and Lighthouse. It was 1970s music that utilized the trumpet, saxophone, trumpet, and trombone players from the school's marching band. It was a seven-piece group, and we used to rehearse in my parents living room.

Sunrise made an awful racket, and the next-door neighbor would call the police every single day complaining about the noise. The police would arrive, tell us to turn it down, and then leave us to resume practicing at same volume as before.

Steve Lozowski was the bass player, lead singer, and songwriter of Sunrise and two grades ahead of me. I was the punk kid. I was an ugly duckling, he was a high school swan: good-looking, talented, cool, hip. The girls all wanted to date him, the boys all wanted to be like him.

He opened a door for me to play keyboards for Sunrise. Our first gig in 1973 was opening for Ezra, another local group at Saint Joseph's High School in Montvale, New Jersey for over 2,500 people. I wore a cape and huge boots as was the outfit of those 70s glam rock days, and we opened with "Magical Mystery Tour." The screaming sound of thousands of people, coupled with how good we sounded through a huge sound system blew my socks off. It felt like a musical version of a full – body orgasm.

If I had any doubts about pursuing a career in music, they were removed after that first gig. Playing music was my fix, my drug. Steve became my best friend, and I looked up to him as a band mate, colleague, and mentor.

However, after we finished high school, our lives paths couldn't have gone in more opposite directions. He went down to the Jersey shore to play in a series of cover bands. He slid into a spiral of harder drugs and being naturally good looking, bedding lots of women. I joined the group Fandango just after they got a huge career break by signing to RCA Records, and my career shot up like a rocket overnight.

Over the next few years all the stories I had heard about Steve were sad and sadder. I heard about arrests, broken friendships, addictions, poverty, and overdoses. Sometime in the early 2000s he surfaced again in my life.

He had been a homeless person for quite a long time. I was told he had five children with four different women, some of whom he never had married. I was told through friends that his children had grown up either never knowing their father, or severely despising him.

I was his last resort. I represented everything that could go right in a local musician's life. To him at least, I was the one that made it. I toured the world, released records, pursued my dream, and worked with many of the talented artists we'd grown up listening to.

Steve arrived at my door one day requesting money to buy new clothing and try to work for a mutual high school friend. I took this one step further. The next day I arranged for him to be admitted to a rehab center in upstate New York. The next thirty days were like witnessing someone awakening from a coma. The old Steve emerged again, clearer of mind, humble, fragile but yet resilient. After a month he was offered a free place at a halfway house, and he set about re-entering the world.

Only it wasn't meant to last. Now I understand someone with a life-threatening addiction that took years to develop also needs many months of rehab, even up to a year, before the fog of addiction even begins to lift. One month was simply too short a time.

Before long, Steve began to complain about the people at the halfway house, many of whom had been released from prison on drug treatment plans. Eventually he stopped attending 12-step meetings. Before long he was homeless and living outdoors again, a grown man in his forties with four children whom he couldn't provide for.

I believe his last conversation was with me before he died. It was the night of July 15th, 2001, under a full moon. I was at the beach having dinner with my yoga teacher. He called me from a homeless shelter near New York's Port Authority Bus Station. He sounded lonely and despondent. He asked me for more money. I simply said I was out of town and would meet up with him when I got back to the city.

The next day I got a call from his sister Karen telling me that he had taken forty sleeping pills that night. His heart stopped, and he quietly passed. My hero, my best friend from high school whom I had once idolized died, at just forty-four years of age in a homeless shelter near the bus terminal.

They say the great tragedy in life is not to have tried and failed, but *to die with the music inside you.* Steve never succeeded early on, or lived long enough to hearing his songs released on a record. He died with the music inside him.

Since I had reconnected over the years with our other band mate Jeff Lee, I asked Jeff to dig through his basement tapes to locate a song that Steve had written. I wanted to pay homage to him, do something to add to his legacy, in other words, to be of service. That's why I chose…

"Journey Through Life"

The interesting part about this song lies within the intersection of its inspiration and service. Steve's favorite band growing up was Chicago. In Sunrise we used to play many of their hits: "Saturday in the Park," "Beginnings," "Feeling Stronger Every Day," "Just You and Me," "25 or 6 to 4."

In my travels as a professional songwriter I'd become friendly with one of Chicago's lead singers Robert Lamm. So I called up Robert, and simply asked if he would be willing to sing harmony on a song for my solo album. I didn't tell him who it was for or anything, just to come and sing. Robert immediately said yes. Then I called my friend Jeff Lee and ask him if he would like to come sing on the record. He was ecstatic. Then I told him he would be singing with Robert Lamm. I swear I could hear Jeff's jaw hit the floor through the phone.

There is something unexplainably surreal to be singing "Saturday in the Park" by Chicago in High School and then finding oneself years later 'dueting' with its composer and lead vocalist.

The day of the session, Robert came in like a true professional. He is world-class all the way. He was on time, down to earth, and simply said,, "Just direct me, tell me what to sing and I'll do it." But he did more than that. When Jeff Lee arrived, Jeff was noticeably nervous meeting his childhood idol. Robert immediately put him at ease, and in fact improvised and directed Jeff to sing a couple of lines with a more creative interpretation that didn't exist originally.

Jeff Lee and Robert Lamm of Chicago

It was only after we finished that I told Robert the truth. Robert, like many people in the music world, had seen too many colleagues lose their talent, career, or even their lives because of the perplexing curse of addiction. Now, here Robert was singing this song written by a person who had the curse of addiction rob him of his life far too young. It was for me, the ultimate tribute and way of giving back, being of service to the memory and spirit of Steve, with Jeff and Robert as angels to the right and left as support. I am forever grateful to Robert Lamm for being so noble and generous. He didn't have to come sing, but he understands the life enhancing power of being of service.

In choosing to record this song, it was to ensure for the future that my dear friend from childhood had left some music behind – some kind of legacy, if you will. To ensure he didn't die with all the music inside him, that one song got out and his legacy endures.

We all wish we could stay young

but time stands still for no-one

JOURNEY THROUGH LIFE
Music and Words by: Steve Lozowski and Jeff Lee

Journey through life with all its strife
and morning comes again to us
Could it be that we're just a little older
And thinking more on life?
Don't play games with yourself anymore boy
soon you'll be a man
And I know it's a long, long road
You must be wise and strong oh
And be what you want to be.
We all wish we could stay young
but time stands still for no-one
You can't sit living in the world past
Long forgotten memories will last
Forever and ever again
With so much to live and so much to give
Like the stars above you, you'll shine
forever and ever again
Could it be that we're just a little older
And thinking more on life?
Don't play games with yourself anymore boy
soon you'll be a man
And I know it's a long, long road
You must be wise and strong oh
And be what you want to be.
We all wish we could stay young

but time stands still for no-one
Journey through life with all its strife
and morning comes again…'till then

THE SONG DECONSTRUCTION

It reads to me lyrically like a letter from beyond the grave, instructing a younger person to put away childish things and become an adult. It is a bittersweet message about the circle of life.

This song was written around 1973, so it has that 1970s mellowed-out feel of a song by CSNY, the Eagles, or Poco. There are a lot of major 7th chords which was a popular form at that time as embodied by Steely Dan, Chicago, and others. It's simple melodically, no great tension and release or dramatic leaps here probably because it was written by a couple of teenagers skilled but perhaps not as gifted early on like Lorde or Taylor Swift, to name just a few. The lack of movement melodically, however, provides a strong foundation for vocal harmonies. You can stack up harmony parts, which are easy to create without all the leaps and bends.

Many songs by similar groups of this era, like the Eagles, rely on this simple melody technique.

MELODY

Steve and Jeff were in their mid-teens when they wrote this song, so the melody in my candid opinion reflects their youth, simplicity and inexperience. The notes often simply follow the chords. There are some elegant (there's that math word again) moments of tension and release however.

At the end of the middle 8 section, "forever and ever" the note lands on a G# on the second "ever," against a D chord, creating a powerful harmonic tension, and the "a" of again is an E note against the D chord (a 2nd) to be released on the second half of the word "A-gain," an F# note against a B chord.

Also there is a dance of notes inside and out of the chord during first half of this section. Resting above an E major chord the lyrics "You can't sit living" are all part of the chord. The word in is an A note against the E chord, a suspended fourth.

The word memories is a B note against an A chord, which is the second note of the scale, a tension note. So there is a light dance of notes that sound very simple melodically, but move just enough to add a tension and release, if ever-so elegantly.

CHORDS

Similar to "Love Heels," the song begins where it ends, with the "Journey through Life" refrain a cappella from the intro but with a full band in the ending section.

The chords are for most part major, happy sounding with few twists and turns. The verse A, E, F# minor is 1, 5, minor 6. It's almost the famous 1, minor 6, 4, 5 sequence, just reversed.

Popular with the jazz rock bands of the day are slight twists and turns. The second line of verse changes A, G# minor to C#. The middle eight or bridge section is the only section of the song that begins on a minor, A# minor. This is very unusual for a pop song these days. To go from A# minor to A, B, G# minor, A, F# minor, B, E. It's a very elegant yet simple round of chords similar to pop jazz forms.

PRODUCTION

After the turbulent times of 1960s and early 1970s with Vietnam, the civil rights movement, Watergate, the singer-songwriters of early 70's were simply trying to mellow out and bring their audience with them. I intentionally set out to capture the freewheeling, more innocent-sounding times of that era with this production. It's a mixture of live and synthesized instruments, performed and co-produced handily by my friend Ben Butler.

I grew up a fan of the group Chicago. This, however, didn't even stop me from thinking twice when it came time to ask Robert Lamm to sing. He sang lead on lines "You can't sit living in a world past, long forgotten memories will last, forever and ever again." I jumped right in after him and sang "With so much to live, so much to give…"

and didn't think twice until afterwards that I'd just sung leads next to a man whom I looked up to as a rock god when I was growing up.

The openness and strumming of electric and acoustic guitars give the song an airy, if somewhat dated feel. It's intended to sound like a period piece. With the recent success of younger bands like the Fleet Foxes, all that's old sounds new again and it has a fresh cultural currency.

Vocally, I was influenced by CSNY with Graham Nash's parts being usually the top falsetto note, so on this track I naturally gravitated toward the high notes and left the lower notes for Robert and Jeff. Growing up my voice went through a particularly challenging register change and I was advised by vocal coaches to give it a rest. If anyone tells me not to do something, being a contrarian by nature I naturally want to do whatever it is, immediately and at least once. Frequently, this didn't yield good results, including being a singer in the groups I had played with early in my career.

I'd be given a microphone to sing harmonies, or a few leads in band after band, only to have the microphone mysteriously vanish when I showed up after a few gigs. I was continually off pitch for years until I started practicing yoga and chanting. Only then could I distinguish my own voice within a much louder environment of singers around me and stay on the correct pitch.

So, singing on this track was like a musical graduation day.

POP SECRET #5: "DON'T BORE US, START WITH THE CHORUS!"

A technique many hit songwriters use is starting with some variation of the chorus as the intro. Why wait? Why not subliminally plant the melody, feel, and mood of the chorus into the listener's ear in zero to ten seconds, instead of after a minute?

Just as in the previous song, which began with "Journey through life with all its strife" sung as an a cappella chorus, songs like "She Loves You" by the Beatles just start rip-roaring full on with the chorus. We love the song in first three seconds! Sold! By the time the verse is finished and we're back into the chorus, we're singing along.

Other composers and producers will offer some tease, a coming attraction of the chorus. On "The Time Of My Life" from the Dirty Dancing soundtrack, Bill Medley sings "I've had the time of my life" over the intro that is in half time and his lead vocal is a full octave lower that the main chorus. This way when the beat comes in the verse lifts up, and when the first chorus hits and Mr. Medley sings an octave higher with a full tenor voice, we find ourselves singing along. Hooked by the hook!

Other teaser/coming attraction-type techniques include merely hinting at the melody. An example of this is "You Give Love a Bad Name" by Bon Jovi. It starts with the guitar weaving around the notes of the chorus melody. It hints at what's to come in the chorus. When the chorus arrives, we intuitively feel somehow we know it, and we're on the hook.

Record your own notes here:

_____
_____
_____
_____
_____
_____
_____
_____
_____
_____

CHAPTER 7. TRUST YOURSELF

Do something each day for yourself. A walk, a bike ride, a yoga class, something that connects you to that quiet voice within.

That voice often knows what your conscious mind doesn't, and it often leads you to wonderful breakthroughs. Many of the world's most successful people from all walks of life attribute their success to trusting their gut. To hear your gut requires listening. For it's the heart, not the mind, that is speaking.

"The journey of a thousand miles begins with a single step."
– Laozi

"With great love all things are possible." *– Sharon Gannon, Jivamukti Yoga*

MY "TRUST YOURSELF" STORY

I didn't know where I was heading. I didn't know what life would hold in store for me. By age twenty-four I felt dazed and confused, like I'd been kicked in the head by a horse named Rock n' Roll. I had toured with my band for three years and had played on stages across North America with some of the biggest stars of the day. I had already been on the covers of magazines, on radio and television.

Yet after four albums Fandango failed to have a hit. The band broke up, and I was floundering trying to launch a solo career.

I had to step into the unknown and face my fears. I had to leave my childhood home and learn to stand on my own two feet. So the song "I Can't Hold You Forever" represents the "trust yourself" key of DWYL, which is vital to any successful enterprise. Be it personal, career, romantic, creative, there is always a huge risk of failure. I simply had to trust that somehow things would be okay.

Once we let go of one thing, often something much better comes along. How many of us are like this – afraid to let go? More often than not, I am.

I wrote this song about my mom, Shirley Friedman Dvoskin. My brother had moved out when he was eighteen and never looked back. There I was, his baby brother still living at home at the age of twenty-four.

It was time to leave the nest, spread my wings and learn to fly. My mom had suffered with loneliness after her divorce, and the pressure of raising two kids. Back in those days, being single with children was looked down upon. Sometimes she would crack under all the pressure, so I had become mother's little helper.

I knew that leaving would be a huge loss for her. Empty nest syndrome causes parents to suffer depression, even when they have a partner and an active life. I knew that in order to find myself, become an adult, I had to leave her all alone in that beautiful house I had grown up in.

I had no healthy choice but to cut the cord. All of life is like a leaf on flowing water downstream through life we go, each moment melts like snow.

I CAN'T HOLD YOU FOREVER

Words and Music by: Larry Dvoskin
I can't hold you forever
hearts can change like the weather
just remember the times we shared,
please know my heart is there
I might not have a reason,
love can change like the season
nothing's real except the here and now
let's make the most of it somehow
I Can't Hold You Forever
hearts can change like the weather
I Can't Hold You Forever

So come on, right now
Come on and hold me tonight
You have changed now you're different
washed along by the current
downstream through life we flow
each moment melts like snow…
I Can't Hold You Forever
hearts can change like the weather
I Can't Hold You Forever
So come on, right now
Come on and hold me tonight

THE SONG DECONSTRUCTION

This lyric is a good-bye letter from a child to their parent. It's a "thank you, I may be gone, but you are always in my heart." It's masked inside a love song so that listeners get to project their own personal story onto the blank screen of this musical canvas.

The lyric can mean a lover to one person, a child to the next, a best friend to yet another person. It's designed specifically to be unspecific. It is yet another example of happy music, bittersweet lyric.

The line "hearts can change like the weather" is not exactly Shakespearean, but it is my favorite image in the song.

The "downstream through life we flow" is of course a reference to "row, row, row your boat," and "each moment melts like snow" is again one of my favorite images.

MELODY

This song is another example of why songwriting is a mysterious art that is challenging to teach. For every so called rule anyone puts forth, there are a multitude of exceptions.

This song definitely breaks out of my theory of tension and release, or bold headline melody. It mostly follows the chords note for note in almost nursery-rhyme fashion. It stridently breaks the concept I set forth deconstructing "Somewhere over the Rainbow" or "Yesterday."

Shirley Girlie – my mom at Coney Island beach, holding a deck of cards. The last time I saw her, before her death in 2004, we played cards.

Yet for some reason, this song stuck in my head, year after year, across decades until I finally recorded it. The synth riff at the beginning with the dotted triplet feel DDD DDD GG F#F# CCC CCC DDD DDD (these are the exact notes), correspond to the verse melody, creating a mantra-like repetition which by the end of the song is sticky. You remember it.

CHORDS AND ARRANGEMENT

The chords are a variation on 1, minor 6, 4, 5.

The verse is a basic 1, 4, 5 = G, C, D major. The chorus starts with the minor 6, E minor, and does a walk down-type riff encompassing the other chords in this progression E minor, D, C, G/B, A minor, D.

The bridge uses a slight variation, B minor, E Minor, C, G, B major, E minor, C, G, D. It provides the basis for a wailing guitar solo in the classic 80s rock style of Journey.

PRODUCTION

I was highly influenced by the English synth bands of the early and mid-1980s. The keyboard riff recreates the style of that era: The Police, Flock of Seagulls, Depeche Mode, etc.

The tempo is this song is a shuffle in 6/8. I was influenced by the Tears for Fears song "Everybody Wants to Rule the World," which has a riff at the beginning that is also a hook.

I wanted a deliberately retro sound: Big reverb drum machine snare drum, analog and digital synths, a wailing 80s guitar solo.

The guitars play the pumping 8th note part that many songs from this era employed. While the guitar is doing 8th notes, the bass below it is playing more sustained notes. When the bridge solo section comes in, the rhythm guitars play sustained power chords thus freeing the bass to play pumping 8th notes. A constant switch up that keeps the energy moving.

THE SEGUE

The segue of this song on "Life Is Strange" into the final track "Each One of Us" has significance too. How does one follow a retro 80s pop song with a very ethereal rock ballad? I was very influenced by Pink Floyd's Dark Side of The Moon. The album was on the Billboard Top 200 album chart for more than a decade. What is so creative is the musical threads that tie each composition together.

Sound effects, noises, echoed voices, an airplane taking off, a wailing voice, gurgling synths made the whole album into a tapestry of different colors, and when finished you wanted to play the album again and again.

So, I wanted to segue out of this wonderful 1980s pop song into something else, otherwise the songs on "Life Is Strange" wouldn't fit together. It would be too much of a hodgepodge.

It adds just the right amount of primordial drama. At times I listen to this segue and dream. I close my eyes and imagine the tunnel of light people say they walk through between this life and the next.

I also used this segue piece of music in the intro of the music video for "Everyone's a Hooker." There's a shot where the camera shifts to reveals a cluster of carnival-like characters all in costume. A priest, a Harry Potter type, a doctor, a lawyer, a little man dressed as Uncle Sam … also a nurse, a football coach, and a musician with a knowing smile, (because that musician…is me).

The message for "I Can't Hold You Forever" is that life itself is passing, impermanent.

POP SECRET #6: SONGS FROM DREAMS

True, we can't control this. But it sure feels good knowing about it when the morning comes.

Some of the most famous songs come to their composers during a dream. There are many examples over the years. Keith Richards talks about hearing the guitar riff from "Satisfaction" in a dream, then waking up and recording it, as he mentioned in his amazing memoir *Life*.

Sting tells the story of hearing "Every Breath You Take" in a dream. The most famous dream story of all is Paul McCartney receiving "Yesterday" in a dream and writing the placeholder lyric "Scrambled Eggs" to it originally.

My own versions of hearing a song idea from a dream, then waking up to figure it out are "Brothers and Sisters" and "Reflexology."

POP SECRET #7: IF IT STICKS WITH YOU, STICK WITH IT!

Which of your songs stick in your head over time?

"I Can't Hold You Forever" was an unfinished song that I'd play in private for decades. For my own enjoyment either alone or in public, I just kept coming back to it. It was always fun, easy, a joy to play.

As a producer, very often people hire me to wade through their songs written over the course of a lifetime, and pick the best ones. I usually ask "which ones do you play by yourself, just for fun?" Or, "Which three songs does everyone like the best?"

We usually know which songs are our best. Yet we want to believe there's an undiscovered gem, a needle in the haystack waiting for someone to discover it.

On "Life Is Strange", almost every song was written over the slow, steady churn of time. These are the songs I'd play at home all by myself for pure enjoyment: "Life Is Strange," "King of Trite," "Love Heels," "I Can't Hold You Forever," "Each One of Us."

"Each One of Us" covered in Chapter 3 is the granddaddy of "stick with you" original songs in my own life. It took hold and cried in my ear like a baby for almost twenty-five years until I finally recorded it and shared it with the public, and now with all of you.

Record your own notes here:

CHAPTER 8. EMBRACE THE NEGATIVE!

Kali (The Hindu God) is the destroyer that breaks things down, so they can be rebuilt stronger and better.

The ache. The divine human condition. We are born, and like sand in an hour glass the whole drama of life plays out – the joy and pain, health and sickness, youth and age as we journey forth through time. The feelings that are expressed in bittersweet songs like "Yesterday" tug at a rich deep chord inside each of us. I wrote my own bittersweet song as I was finishing up the writing of this book.

MY "EMBRACE THE NEGATIVE" STORY

While finishing up the editing for *Do What You Love*, explaining all the *follow your joy, good leads to better, see life as energy* Pollyanna type concepts, my life was unexpectedly torpedoed and I felt capsized. I suddenly didn't know where I was heading. I didn't know what life would hold in store for me.

After years of comfortable living in New York City's Greenwich Village renting an apartment in the same building Jimi Hendrix once called home, I found myself under attack. One of the neighbors who up until then was my best friend for years on the same floor, suddenly had a falling out with me. She went from best friend who shared birthday parties, Thanksgiving and Christmas dinners in my home, being part of the 'soul family' I never had, to leading a campaign behind my back to have me evicted.

In New York City a board of residents owns many buildings, and the city is famous for mini wars that act themselves out as board members flex their powers over others, sometimes for the greater good, other times for their own ego or agenda. She also while serving on the board of the building, acted informally as the buildings prime real estate agent, often getting first dibs and a heads up on vacancies. Seven months after I moved out, the apartment was rented and an agent received a tidy commission. You might take a guess who the agent listing the apartment was?

I had no idea that since I moved in in 1998 I was being lucky or protected from any undue attention from the board. It was a free flowing decade and a half of a creative Greenwich Village New York life: musicians coming over to jam, write songs, parties, guests, a whole array of "doing what I love."

Suddenly I received lawyers' letters, threatening that I was in violation of rules. Neighbors, staff, and friendly board members came forward to tell me that three women including the neighbor mentioned above, which one resident described as "The Witches of Eastwick," had their fangs and claws out for me in their mind at least, to create a vacancy. It felt like death by a thousand paper cuts as they needled the owner of my apartment constantly anytime I fell outside of building rules. Rules that I had imagined I was following for 15 years as no one ever previously had complained. In fact, my behavior had grown more conservative over time as I focused more on my work.

I felt attacked, bullied, picked on. Even worse than that feeling was the fact that my former best friend told me she was on my side, but it was others lined up against me when numerous neighbors close to the situation told me the opposite was true.

How was I to write this book about "follow your joy," "good leads to better," "be audacious," "trust yourself" when I was feeling so horrible, so depressed, sad, alone, empty inside? That is the truest test of Doing What You Love. How does one stay grateful and positive in the midst of pain, loss, tragedy? I felt afraid of being a phony here and saying how I have all the answers, when really the challenge to "Do What I Hate" felt SO strong.

I have learned in life that one of the main secrets is to go where I am celebrated, not tolerated. So, as hard as it was in 2013 and 2014 while writing and editing this book, I learned to *embrace the negative* – that when I trust life, life will take care of me, though sometimes through painful circumstances.

I had to embrace the negativity by flowing along with rather than trying to deny, fight or control events out of my control. I had to step into the unknown and face my fears. So the song "Live It All" represents the bonus key of how to face the challenges that come up in life, be they death, hunger, hardship, poverty, sickness, heartbreak.

This key is about how to not give in to the 'fight or flight' survival instinct of "Do What You Hate." I simply had to take one step at a time, have faith and know that somehow things would be okay.

Once we embrace the negativity by letting go of one thing, often something much better comes along.

LIVE IT ALL
Words and Music by: Larry Dvoskin

I've got to live,
live by my own rules
I've got to fall,
when falling's the ignorance of fools
I've got to feel,
with all of my soul when love comes to call
I've got to Live – To Live It All
I've got to strive,
in a whole world of things that I'm not
I've got to fight,
fight to hold on to the things that I've got
I've got the sun,
streaming through branches that will fall
I've got to Live – To Live It All
ba, ba, ba, ba, ba – ba
I've got to win,
when the odds are a million to one
just to be alive,
be called my momma, my poppa's son
I've got to climb,

> climb many mountains, ladders, and walls
> I've got to Live, yes I've got To Give,
> I've got to Live – to Live It All

THE SONG DECONSTRUCTION

As mentioned, I was in pain. I felt like the wind was knocked out of me. So the opening line about "living by my own rules" is about what each artist or innovator faces, living and thinking outside the lines, outside the box.

There is a saying "mediocrity cannot tolerate excellence." I'm not claiming to be extraordinary in this case, but it's a pattern. What makes us exceptional, or disruptive, is threatening to those who only obey the rules.

The "I've got to fall, when falling's the ignorance of fools" directly refers to the women at that time on the condo board.

Mankind's folly is how we harm others out of ignorance. The second line "I've got to fall" was my knowing that sooner or later, like a chisel in the hard stone if they kept needling me, spying and reporting, and sending letters to my very kind and patient landlord, eventually the stone would crack. Little did they know – my favorite saying is "God punishes us by answering our prayers" and the events would be immortalized in this song.

The second verse of "I've got to strive, in a whole world of things that I'm not, I've got to fight, fight to hold onto the things that I've got," refers to my wallow in feeling sorry for myself. It got me to thinking about the 15 years of life lived out, chances missed, loves lost, fortunes spent. The fight in this case was simply to not allow people with an agenda, dictate my life. I did fight to hold onto what I've got and after the building agents sent a secret letter to my owner saying in essence "throw Larry under the bus," he replied "I am standing by him and renewing his lease. If you have a problem with that, contact his attorney."

The "sun steaming through branches that will fall," is perhaps my favorite line. It speaks to the fact that all things are impermanent. The sun, the green branch, everything is in a state of change; a constant flux of rise and fall, growth and decay.

"I've got to win, when the odds are a million to one, just to be alive and be called my momma, my poppa's son." The statistical odds of being alive are so astronomical, I've read somewhere in the fertilization process of egg and sperm, it's more like 250,000,000 to 1. But that number just doesn't sing well. I have to always remember what a blessing life is. And the road ahead doesn't have to look like the road left behind. I heard a great line today from a friend: "it's okay to look back, but don't stare." "I've got to climb, climb many mountains, ladders and walls" refers to the hope, and optimism that after the darkest hour there is always a new day, a new chance, a new adventure.

CHORDS

1, 5, Minor 6, 4. Here it is yet again. You can sing "With or Without You" by U2, or the chorus of Lady Gaga's "Paparazzi" over the verse of "Live It All," as it's the exact same chord pattern. The only difference here is the tempo is a 6/8 feel and much slower. During the second half of the verse – it opens up a bit musically and melodically. It goes 4, 5, minor 6, and then major second (just to mix it up), then back to 4, 5, and 1. The melody soars on the 4 chord, a D major and is an F# which again contradicts the tension and release theory somewhat, as it's within the chord. A note that stands out more is on the word "live" in the last line, title line. It's a major seventh, which lends to a very pretty sound, which contrasts to the rock & blues notes throughout the verses.

ARRANGEMENT AND PRODUCTION

The song is a shuffle in 6/8 time. And it's a different type of shuffle than "I Can't Hold You Forever" whose dotted note feel is reminiscent of Tears for Fears "Everybody wants to Rule The World." This type of beat and feel is more old Americana blues, as exemplified by the sounds of Muscle Shoals studios in 1960's and 1970's; the mix of white and black influence.

I was fortunate to have a stellar line up of musicians assemble to record it: Chuck Burgi on drums, who plays with Billy Joel; Royston Langdon on bass, who is the front man of art rock band Spacehog;

Hugh Pool who was inducted into the Blues Hall of Fame of NYC on guitar, and the amazingly talented singer/songwriter Sam Kogon. I wanted that clean guitar arpeggio part heard on early soul records. The feel of these musicians locked in immediately and each take was pretty amazing and great.

In July of 2015 for a week I stayed in the lush green of nature at a friend's guesthouse in Katonah, New York. On a dusty, out of tune spinet piano I finished the melody and lyrics. The piano seemed to have a soul, like the spirit of a brave Indian shaman that whispered in my ear as I spent days and nights alone. I sang the lead vocal the following week at Avatar Studios in New York City. A studio where The Rolling Stones, Bruce, U2, Bon Jovi and so many others created music which touched the world. I brought along my NYU songwriting students who witnessed as I sang lead and the amazing Audrey Martells sang the background vocals. What a gift!

BRIDGE

The bridge is clearly the influence of Al Jardine of The Beach Boys who has been my co-writing and producing partner for many years. It's unexpected. Three minor chords in a row, ascending and the second and third being chromatic, which means right next to each other.

The vocals try to emulate sections of "God Only Knows" or "Good Vibrations," lots of layering and just notes from low to high trading off with each other. This gives the section an entirely different feeling from the rest of the song which is rather simple, direct, and soulful.

ENDING

I love last chorus ride outs. Meaning we've had a satisfying experience with the song, both to our ears and hopefully hearts and there is often an expansion which happens after the last chorus. Think "Hey Jude" where it segues into the iconic "Na, na, na, na na na, na's." In "Live It All" the chords are 1, 5, minor 6, 4 where the vocalist gets to improvise soulfully repeating the title of the song.

I am in a pattern lately of leavings my songs hanging on a chord that feels unresolved, so instead of ending on the 1 chord, in this case an A chord, it ends on the 4 which is a D chord. It leaves the door open like a sequel, like in film franchises. It's finished, but not completely over. I do the same technique on a number of songs examined in this book, "Life Is Strange," "Love Heels," "King of Trite." Perhaps I am a serial un-resolver?

Or perhaps, there is still another lyric, another melody, another song waiting to be born within us that is floating on the air like a wistful hummingbird's wing? Per chance there is yet another song that we may one day leave behind as a gift for future generations to be inspired from the time capsule of our brief and fleeting moments here on Earth?

I've lived this question, and perhaps one day may grow into the answer.

Record your own notes here:

AFTERWORD

After releasing the e-book "Do What You Love – Songwriting" in September of 2014 on Amazon and my own website, the most wonderful things began happening.

People across the world came out of the woodwork to help. A woman in New Zealand printed up a dozen copies at her own expense and mailed physical copies to me. A major movie company lent their production studio to me for free to so I could create and edit DWYL life lesson videos. We started having 'salons' at various apartments in New York City where people gathered to share their dreams and ask for support, ideas, or contacts. I began teaching Do What You Love – Songwriting at New York University, and The Rock and Roll Fantasy Camp. A community gathered online to post inspiring thoughts, as well as their challenges or personal breakthroughs. And quite wonderfully people started buying the e-book without any big publisher marketing, or promoting it.

Now there is an increasing number of what I call glass half empty experts who bemoan the whole notion of Do What You Love as dangerous, hedonistic. An author Miya Tokumitsu even wrote a book titled "Do What You Love and other Lies About Success and Happiness." Totally negating authors like Joseph Campbell, Norman Vincent Peale, Dale Carnegie, and many other leading thinkers of modern age, Tokumitsu argues that corporate interests have co-opted the concept of do what you love in order to exploit employees. That menial jobs don't offer happiness, and we should all be realistic because there are less jobs for a career you may be passionate about, than there are people who share that passion. While this may be true, I would rather try and fail, than live a life of quiet desperation and never try. To repeat the Albert Einstein quote in the introduction "The tragedy of life is what dies inside a man while he lives." Life is short. We never know how much time we have on this planet. By choosing to NOT HAVE A FALLBACK POSITION, either make it or die trying; that passion has led me to an extraordinary, joy filled life full of meaning. By me simply doing what I love, and sharing my insights for the benefit of others, I found a personal measure of success more precious than rubies.

If you have an idea to help promote or market this book, wish to arrange for a reading, workshop, master class, or have an idea to pitch for future books in this Do What You Love series, please contact us at todayisthefuture@gmail.com

Life is limitless possibility.

Good luck and blessings on your journey.

GLOSSARY OF TERMS

DWYL – Do What You Love

Hook – "A catchy memorable part of the song." It might be the chorus, or a repeating "la, la, la, la, la." It might be the guitar riff at the beginning of "Layla" by Eric Clapton, or the synth melody in MGMT's "Kids." It's the part of the song that once it gets in your ear, it is hard to get rid of it.

Chorus – The part of a song that the verse, and the pre chorus builds up to. Often doubles as the hook, a memorable, sometimes repeating of one phrase like "I Will Always Love You." It's like the head on the body of the song.

Verse – Most often where the singing starts, the part that tells the story. Often in pop music it's 4 bars or 8 bars after the beginning and lasts for 8 bars.

Measure/ Bars – a unit of beats. Most commonly 4 beats to a measure/bar, but can be 3, 5, 6, etc.

Bridge/Middle 8 – refers to the part of the song that varies away from the rest of the song, gives the listener a break from the repeating patterns of verse, chorus, verse, or chorus. The term middle 8 is an English term which means the bridge, and refers to the usual length of the section being 8 bars long.

B verse/Pre chorus – is the section just before the chorus. Often it's a variation of the verse that builds up in feeling, intensity, preparing the listener for a musical explosion or release into the chorus. Usually it is 4 measures in length.

Riff – a series of notes. It could mean a vocal improvisation happening during the end of a song or over a layer of background harmonies. It can also be instrumental as in an instrument melody such as a guitar or keyboard adding contrast or emotion to a musical section.

Click/Metronome – an electronic sound generated to help the musicians stay in the exact *beats per minute* (BPM) tempo throughout the song.

Pan/Panning – placing instruments or sounds to the right or left.

Legato – a smooth held note or sound

Staccato – a sharp, short note or sound.

2nd, 3rd, 4th 5th, 6th, 7th, 8 – relates to the note of the musical scale 1) do, 2) re, 3) mi 4) fa 5) sol 6) la 7) ti 8) do!

Minor or Major 2nd, 3rd, 4th, 5th, etc. – determines whether the note or chord being discussed is in a major or minor key.

Whole Note – one note for each beat.

8th Note – a note lasting for ½ of a beat= 2 notes per beat.

16th note – 4 notes per beat.

Dotted 8th triplet – beats are usually divided into even numbers twos and fours. However, an 8th note triplet is where 3 notes are played instead of 2, creating a galloping staggered feeling.

www.ingramcontent.com/pod-product-compliance
Ingram Content Group UK Ltd.
Pitfield, Milton Keynes, MK11 3LW, UK
UKHW062045180426
11947UKWH00030B/2057